From Hell to Paradise

From Hell to Paradise

Soraya Fathi Bazyar

Translated by: Dr Iraj Master
Edited by: Ms. Dawn Tahirih Vojdani

To order additional copies of this book, contact:
Xlibris Corporation
1-888-795-4274
www.Xlibris.com
Orders@Xlibris.com
67010

Contents

Preface

This story is dedicated to the Australian Government, Australian Community and the Human Rights Organisations as a token of my heartfelt thanks and appreciation. Year after year they have supported and provided refuge for thousands of refugees from all over the world.

These refugees in reality are sacrificial lambs of religious, racial, ethnic and political fanaticism in their own lands. To save their lives from impending life threatening, persecutions and cruelties, they have been forced to abandon their own homes, confront other dangers in order to find and eventually settle in a safe place.

Soraya Fathi Bazyar a religious refugee with a deep sympathy for other refugees, outlines some of the pains and sufferings, on the path towards freedom and security with this factual story based on life experience.

My deepest and sincerest wishes for the establishment of peace and security around the world.

Prologue

Since Iran's Islamic Revolution in 1979, many major events have greatly influenced the destiny of numerous Iranians. The event that changed the direction of our lives, started with the sudden and unexpected invasion of our home by revolutionary guards. After much danger and enduring adventures, it ended in freedom from oppression and settling in a foreign and hospitable land.

First Years of the Revolution

It was a summer day late in June 1984. It was very hot and the school holidays had started. Our home was located in the Zargandeh Hills, a suburb of Tehran. It was about five o'clock in the afternoon and the neighbours had returned from work and were gathered in the alley to have a neighbourly chat, exchange the daily news and gossip, or complain about the land, the heaven and their worries.

Unfortunately, in those days the news was not particularly good, but rather heart-breaking. It was mainly about the war between Iran and Iraq, the bloodshed of Iranian youth on Iraqi's mine-fields, the arrest of a fellow citizen who opposed the present regime, and the jailing and killing of Bahá'ís in different parts of the country.

The Bahá'ís form the largest religious minority in Iran. Religious superstitions had overtaken the public in the 19th Century in Iran, and the reality of the Islamic teachings and principles had been forgotten. In the middle of this Century, namely in 1844, a Young Man Whose title was the Báb, which means "Gate", claimed that He was the Herald of a new religion, the Bahá'í Faith.

He invited the people to welcome the Manifestation of a new religion with universal teachings and principles for the whole world. A great number of religious leaders, Islamic nobility, and intellectuals accepted His claims.

Day by day His followers grew in number. Like other Prophets of the past, such as Moses, Jesus and Muhammad, the Báb was mistreated by the Islamic clergy, the ignorant rulers and the government officials of the time, and He was finally executed in 1850 at the age of 31 by a firing squad in the city of Tabríz in north western Iran.

After the Báb, Bahá'u'lláh, Who was from a noble family and the son of one of the Government ministers, fulfilled the Báb's prophecy as the Founder of a new universal religion.

Bahá'u'lláh abandoned His comfort, wealth and high status. He invited the people to new teachings and principles. His teachings are based on the acceptance of the oneness of God, the oneness of religion, and the oneness and equality of all humanity. These principals would require the removal of all religious, racial and other prejudices.

He founded a religion that is based on love and harmony amongst people. Like previous Prophets, Bahá'u'lláh was harshly treated by the religious leaders, the people, and the government.

He was exiled from His home country, Iran, to a prison city called 'Akká, under the Ottoman Empire, where He spent 40 years of His earthly life and from where His holy soul ascended to the spiritual Kingdom.

During His exile and imprisonment, Bahá'u'lláh proclaimed His teachings, guidance and exhortations for a new and united world to the Kings and Rulers, and the peoples of the world.

At present, Bahá'ís of different nationalities, religious and other racial backgrounds reside in more than 200 countries in the world and work unitedly for a better future for mankind.

It is unfortunate to note that from its inception in Iran Bahá'ís have been subject to extreme mistreatment, cruelty, and constant harassment, and they have been deprived of their social and human rights.

— — — — — — — — — — — —

In those days the good news amongst the neighbours was about being able to purchase a kilo of meat, a bag of rice, or a dozen eggs. And that was only possible if you had grocery coupons, then you could go to the grocer, Abbás Ághá, or to the butcher, Asgar Ághá, in the neighbourhood shops. Even then you needed to be at the head of the queue, otherwise you would return home empty-handed.

Our neighbours came from different political, religious and other schools of thought. They were generally middle class citizen like traders, government employees, army officers, bazaar merchants, and builders. They all lived in the neighbourhood with mutual respect and harmony. However, in those days it was unlikely to find anyone who was happy and refreshed because they were all obliged to adjust themselves to the new laws and philosophy that were then ruling the community. Every neighbour whinged and expressed his or her dissatisfaction one way or another. They all hoped that soon a saviour would emerge who would topple the government.

One of the very fashionable and stylishly dressed ladies of our area, who was fed up with the Islamic dress code and tired of wearing so many layers of clothes in such hot weather said: "Instead of forcing me to cover myself, why don't they educate our Islamic brothers to look at women with clean and chaste eyes, just like they look at their own sisters? Besides, are belief and chastity dependant upon wearing a veil and a burka? Let them go and discover how some people commit detestable acts under their veils. I am waiting for the downfall of this government; I know what I will do then. I will undress myself completely, walk down the streets, and take revenge against such stupid enforced covering of the body."

One of the neighbours at the end of the alley had lost her young son in the war with Iraq. The religious group from the local mosque held a memorial gathering for him and mourned loudly, beating their chests. They called him a martyr and changed the name of the alley to his name in order to calm the bereaved mother and thus keep her mouth shut. Nobody knew why he was a martyr. A person becomes a martyr to prove a cause.

Islam has proven its divine origin over 14 centuries. Now two Islamic nations, Iran and Iraq, were fighting each other for unknown reasons. Why should a victim of a brutal war become a martyr, for whom or for what cause? Why should two Muslim countries fight and shed each others' blood? What conspiracy is going on behind the scenes? Maybe impartial historians and politicians of the future will be able to explain it.

Another neighbour of ours was the Nazarí family. They were a very polite and friendly family. The head of the family worked for the oil company and the wife was a good friend of mine. During the Shah's regime she used to follow the current fashion and wear European-made dresses. It was strange that just before the revolution she went on pilgrimage to Mecca and repented of her past. Now in the streets and the markets she walked around with a veil and Islamic dress. She organised classes on the Qur'án in her home and nobody knew what had caused such a dramatic change in this family. This family presumably worked hard to establish a just, democratic government by removing the Shah's regime.

Another neighbour of ours was a merchant family and believed in observing the Islamic traditions. They were quiet people who were engaged in their own affairs. From the time of the <u>Shah</u> the mother and daughters of the family used to dress of their own volition according to the Islamic rules and they were not of those who would change with the direction of the wind.

Innate nobility and chastity could be seen in this family. One of their daughters was very beautiful and sometimes from my kitchen window I could see her passing by our house and I would admire her beauty. She was a university student who was interested in partisan and political activities. It was in the early years of the Revolution and I had not seen her for a while. One day I asked her mother about her daughter's well-being. She sighed with tears in her eyes and said; "I have had no news from her since she moved out. I hope God will protect her." Later I heard that this family left our area and I never heard from them again; I do not know what might have happened to this girl and her family.

Our other neighbour was the Atoofí family. They had a son in the United States and their younger son was my son Basim's mate. He and a few other boys from the area were a noisy bunch when they played together in the alley.

This family had a large house on the corner of the block and they seemed to be very well off. Mrs. Atoofí went to the United States every summer to visit her son. Sometimes she wore a scarf and other times she appeared in the alley with her hair well coifed.

One morning the residents noticed that on the wall of their house was written "Death to the people of the Savak". (The Savak was the security organization from the time of the <u>Shah</u>). Mrs. Atoofí came out and she was angry and swearing while she removed the writing.

Another neighbour of ours was Mrs. Behnamí. She was about 80 years old, very lively, kind, and full of vitality; she lived alone and felt lonely. She collected stamps and exchanged them with my children. She often spoke about and discussed the value of the stamps for a long time with my children.

She lived in one of the apartments opposite our house. Her balcony overlooked our house. My husband Cyrus and her son had been friends and schoolmates for many years.

We had regular encounters with this lady and she always complained about the noise the kids made in the alley, including my older son Shamim who played volleyball with the other youth in the alley. She used to talk a lot about her back and tooth pains, and her relationship with her daughter-in-law. I would often see her on her balcony and would hear her complaining.

In addition to us, there were three other Bahá'í families who lived in our small alley.

One of them had sent his wife and children to another country. The other family consisted of a young couple who were our next door neighbours who had a young child. They lived very quietly and worked hard.

General Atá'u'lláh Mogharebi (this is his real name), another Bahá'í in the neighbourhood, had an old house at the head of the alley, on the corner. He was a member of the National Spiritual Assembly of Iran who, together with the other members, were kidnapped and never heard of again. His house had been ransacked and confiscated and from time to time we saw the Revolutionary Guards going and coming to and from his house.

Another family who lived in the block of apartments opposite us and with whom we had a very good relationship was Mr. and Mrs. Razaví, who had a girl and a boy.

Mr. Razaví was from Rasht, a city in northern Iran; he was a very honest, intellectual man with integrity, who wished people well, and who was a lover of freedom. My husband Cyrus and I trusted him.

My husband and I often discussed our pains and woes with him and sought his advice. I remember that when my husband was dismissed from the oil company he became very sad and unhappy. Mr. Razaví told my husband; "You could have said one word: that you are a Muslim, then you could have kept your job and would have had a comfortable life." We explained to Mr. Razaví that there is no recanting of our belief in the Bahá'í Faith as this was contradictory to honesty and integrity, and one's heart and tongue should express the same.

We more or less had good relationships with our other neighbours and were aware of their current situations. We would greet each other when we met and during Naw Rúz (the Iranian New Year) we would visit each other; during the Islamic days of mourning we would make *sholeh zard* (a kind of rice pudding with saffron) and send it to each other's house.

Our Muslim neighbours would invite us for the commemoration of the death of his holiness Abbás; we would accept the invitation and listen to the clergy speak about his pain and suffering. While the audiences listened to him, they would cry and unload their pains and problems from their hearts. At the end, food was served and everyone enjoyed each other's company. Almost everybody in our neighbourhood knew that we were Bahá'ís.

During the Shah's reign, the educated and the intellectuals in the larger cities did not care about other people's beliefs, their political orientation or their school of thought.

Unfortunately, even then the ignorant fanatics were often influenced by the hostile discriminating talks of the religious leaders. They would broadcast untrue, slanderous talks against the Bahá'ís over the radio stations and the loudspeakers of the mosques. The people who were influenced by them would attack and mistreat the Bahá'ís. In all these situations, the government and religious clergy policy in Shah time, was to keep the principles and the facts of the Bahá'í Faith under the cover of doubts and obscurity. No mention of the Faith has ever been made in any kind of public meeting or official gathering.

— — — — — — — — — — — — — —

Since the Revolution in 1979, due to their political or religious affiliations, a great number of Iranians have been interrogated, arrested or killed. Just like thousands of other Iranians, the Bahá'ís could not save themselves from this killing field. A lot of them were sacrificed with utmost cruelty by attacks from their enemies, ungodly people and fanatics.

Bahá'ís in every country around the world have administrative bodies called local or national spiritual assemblies that are elected. After the Revolution, members of the national assembly and of many local assemblies were captured, imprisoned, and many of them were executed.

In many towns and villages mobs attacked the Bahá'ís, burned down and looted their houses. They bashed them and forced them to flee from their own homes. They didn't even show any mercy for their animals, they burned them or caused them to run away and die somewhere else. They even attacked and desecrated Bahá'í cemeteries so even dead Bahá'ís lost their place of rest and peace.

In 1983 the news of the arrest, imprisonment and execution of ten Bahá'í women in the Adel-Abad Prison in Shíráz broke our hearts and left an unforgettable scar on our souls. The youngest of these was Mona Mahmudnizad, who was only 17 years old, Akhtar Sabet 21, Roya Eshraghí 22, Simin Saberí 24, Shahín Dalvand 25, Mahshid Niroumand 28, Zarrín Moghimí 29, Tahireh Siavashí 32, Nosrat Yalda'ee 56, and Ezzat Eshraghí 57.

They were mostly young women, chosen because they were teaching Bahá'í children about religion and virtues. They were, of course, accused of being spies, but they would have been acquitted if they had become Muslims and their crimes would have been cleansed (reported in Payam-i-Bahá'í 345-346, 165 Bahá'í Era).

With a bit of justice, one could ask where is this school that produces spies and trains them from primary school age up to men 80 years old. The Bahá'ís are practically spread all over the world and if they are spies, how is it the advanced countries with sophisticated security systems have not accused a single Bahá'í of being a spy? Perhaps these countries are in a deep slumber!

The Bahá'ís in every corner of Iran are gradually being dismissed from work in Government Offices and their lives become harder and harder every day. The superannuation of retired employees has been terminated. Why? Because, based on the Iranian Islamic Fundamentalism, Bahá'ís are heathens and spies. They are not allowed to live and breathe in this country. They have called them a misled sect and deprived of all human rights.

With utmost patience, meekness and forbearance the Bahá'ís suffer these difficulties and never try to avenge themselves. They do not even use arms to defend themselves, because violence and rage are a contradiction of their ideals of peace and love. The Bahá'ís reciprocate anger with love, violence with calm, bitterness with sweetness. They counter ugly words with beautiful words and injury with a healing balm. They always remind themselves of Bahá'u'lláh's words; He said:

O Oppressors On Earth! Withdraw your hands from tyranny, for I have pledged Myself not to forgive any man's injustice. This is My covenant which I have irrevocably decreed in the preserved tablet and sealed with My seal.

— — — — — — — — — — — — — —

After my husband's dismissal from the oil company, our only income was my salary as a teacher in one of the government schools. In addition, we had some saving and by economising we could survive.

During the reign of the Shah, I studied children's education and was employed by the Ministry of Education. I started teaching in a boys' primary school in Majidieh, one of the poor suburbs of Tehran. In those days we also had to mention our religion on our employment papers. Most of the Bahá'ís would not answer this question on their employment application. This was not a problem then. After the Islamic Revolution, I continued teaching at the same school, but I knew that sooner or later I would also join the ranks of dismissed Bahá'ís.

Several times I received questionnaires from the Ministry of Education asking about my income, including my spouse's income, the number of children we had and our bank debts, etc. But strangely, none of them asked about our religious beliefs. I was however, waiting for the occasion to tell them that I am a Bahá'í, wanting to know where I stand. If I had any shortcomings or made any mistakes, they should let me know.

During class breaks I, together with the other teachers, would go to the Headmaster's Office for a tea break and to consult about the children's education and then return to classes.

Our Headmaster was a nice, courageous man who was originally from Kurdestán, a province of Iran. He was a tall, good-looking, serious man with authority. As soon as we told naughty, noisy students that we would report them to the Headmaster, Mr. Farvandí, they would behave themselves.

Whenever the Headmaster, Mr. Farvandí, appeared in the school yard, the students would be quiet and go right to their lines to go into their classrooms. In those days very light corporal punishment was permitted. If kind words and advice was not effective, the children would be hit a few times with a ruler on the palm of their hands. The parents were satisfied with this arrangement and they even asked the Headmaster to be stricter with their children. A few of the students would not respond to any language except corporal punishment. Apparently that is how they were treated in their homes.

The relationship between the teachers was very cordial and caring and each one eagerly focused on their duties. Amongst the teachers there was one whose name was Ms. Shams. Even during the time of the Shah she would wear the Islamic veil (*hejab*), and even the female colleagues never saw one strand of her hair. Actually, she would jokingly say:

"You know what? I am bald and that is why I am wearing a scarf and a veil!"

She was very cheerful and friendly, a talker and like the other teachers, she was skilful at her job. She would not drive a car. Sometimes I used to drive her from the school to the bus stop, where I had the chance to enjoy her company.

A while after the Revolution, Ms. Shams's brother was killed in a local conflict with the Kurds. We were saddened by the news. The authorities honoured her brother as a martyr (*shahíd*) and she received special respect at work and in the community.

Mr. Farvandí, who was a Kurd, lost his position as Headmaster and was transferred elsewhere as a teacher. We were all very sorry and never heard of him again.

He was immediately replaced by Mr. Mahmoodí, a young man with the Islamic appearance of those days, which means a wrinkled suit, a dark shirt, black hair, and unshaven. He always had worry beads in his hand, looking down because the teachers were all women and he and his deputy were the only men.

Seeing him, all the women became very reserved and concerned, they made sure that even their foreheads were covered. The atmosphere at the school and the office changed. We all wished that Mr. Farvandí (the previous Headmaster) would return.

We fantasized that if Mr. Farvandí had also grown a little beard, held worry beads in his hand and gone to Friday prayers at the mosque, he would still be there. But obviously his Kurdish righteousness was far above those cheap, hypocritical tricks. Ms. Shams was now very enthusiastic because there was a new religious Headmaster who was a staunch Muslim like herself.

A few weeks went by and we got to know more about the new Headmaster and we realized that we should not judge people by their outward appearance. I can now say that he was a staunch Muslim who loved his fellow humans. He was free of fanaticism and his aim was to serve, not to make problems for his co-workers. We gradually got used to him and everybody was doing their best at work.

Just like before, I was wondering and was in doubt as to what I should do if the Headmaster should one day find out that I was a Bahá'í. Soon the time of the Nineteen Day Feast arrived. Bahá'ís in every locality attend a meeting every 19 days that is called the "Nineteen Day Feast". The purpose of the Feast is to strengthen the love and unity amongst the Bahá'ís. The first part of the Feast consists of prayers and reciting Holy Writings, followed by consultation and suggestions about the administrative and social affairs of the community. During this part everyone has the chance to offer suggestions or recommendations in relation to local, national or even international affairs. In the third and final part, the Bahá'í friends socialize, enjoy each other's company and the hospitality of the host in whose house the Feast is held.

At the Feast that evening, the Bahá'ís were warned about the situation of the Bahá'ís employed by Government organizations. The rumour was that they would be dismissed or even forced to repay the salaries they had received during the last few years. It was recommended that the Bahá'í friends introduce themselves to their superior officers and ask for their advice.

That night I was thinking all night long about what I should do. How could I bring up this problem with the Headmaster, Mr. Mahmoodí, the sooner, the better? A few days passed and I received my monthly salary. Several times I attempted to talk to him, but he was either out of his office or there were others present. I waited for another opportunity. Another day, after the teachers returned to their classes, I took the opportunity and went to Mr. Mahmoodí's office.

I told him I had a problem that I had to discuss with him. He said; "Fine, but your students are waiting for you in the classroom. You had better go to your class and I will see you there." I returned to my class and continued teaching as usual. After a while there was a knock at the door and Mr. Mahmoodí arrived. The children stood up out of respect. I gave them a small exercise to keep them busy. Mr. Mahmoodí was standing in a corner. I approached him and said:

"By now you may have heard that almost all the Bahá'ís employed by the government have been dismissed from work. Some of them have been arrested and some have been killed. The truth is that I am also a Bahá'í and do not think that my blood is of any greater value than that of my fellow

Bahá'ís who have sacrificed their lives without hesitation. I would like to know your views and those of the office concerning this matter."

Mr. Mahmoodí was looking down as usual and for a few moments he was shocked and motionless. He threw a look at me and said: "Madam, have you recently had any arguments or problems at home with your husband that have made you angry and you are telling me these things due to your anger? You had better think about this and see if you feel the same tomorrow. I will see you in this classroom again tomorrow."

He left the class and I continued teaching with a thousand and one worries in my mind. The next day I went to school as usual and carried on teaching. Somehow I was calm and ready. Mr. Mahmoodí knocked on the door and entered.

He asked me: "What do you think? Are you still a Bahá'í?"

I said, "Yes, I am a Bahá'í."

Then he asked: "Is your husband at work?"

I said, "No, he was an employee of the oil company, but he was dismissed because he is a Bahá'í".

He further asked; "What are you going to do now?"

And continued; "Your husband is out of work and you will also be dismissed, how will you survive?"

I smiled and said: "I do not know, maybe we will sit at the crossroads and sell cooked broad beans and cooked beet roots. God is great! We will do something; we will not die of starvation."

With utmost courtesy and kindness he said: "I have to fulfil my duty. I will go straight to the head of the division and submit my report on you."

I told him that I was happy for him to carry out his duty. Soon after this conversation, he nervously and agitatedly returned to my class and said: "Mrs. Fathi, I am sorry but I was told that under no circumstances are you eligible to teach Muslim children. You should go home right now." That memorable day was 26th January 1983.

I was dumbfounded and did not know what to say. In less than two hours my dismissal orders had been issued and executed. I was not even allowed to finish that day's duties. I said to the Headmaster that, with his permission, I would sit in the school's office until the break so that I could say good-bye to my colleagues. If I suddenly disappeared, my colleagues might think I had committed a crime or something drastically wrong.

Mr. Mahmoodí said all right, I could stay in his office until the next break. One after another my colleagues arrived and, as usual, they enjoyed drinking tea and eating cookies. After a few minutes, in a loud voice I said: "Dear friends, today I want to say good-bye to you forever."

They were all stunned and said: "What? Why? Where are you going?"

I said, "The truth is this: I am a Bahá'í and, as you might have heard, the majority of the Bahá'ís have been dismissed from their government jobs and now it is my turn."

All my colleagues expressed their sorrow and regret, but they couldn't say anything more because they might be accused of being Bahá'í supporters, which could get them into trouble with the authorities.

I walked to each lady colleague and embraced her, kissed her, and said farewell forever. However, when I got close to Ms. Shams, one of teachers I mentioned before, she put her hands in front of her chest, walked back and did not let me hug her, saying; "No, no, Mrs. Fathi." I was shocked and perplexed, and did not know what to do or to say. I very quickly hugged the other few and moved on. The school caretaker, deeply sad, was standing in the hallway, I said good-bye to him and walked quickly out through the school gate and got into my car. I do not know how I got home.

I cried all the way home. I did not cry because of the loss of my job or the money, but because I never received an answer to my questions regarding human rights. I was confident that a Higher Authority gives me my bread, and not the present regime.

My questions were about the rights of an Iranian Bahá'í. Why should an Iranian Bahá'í be treated like someone with the plague or leprosy? Why shouldn't a Bahá'í have the right to ask why? And why couldn't he or she be able to defend his or her rights? My tears were more for Ms. Shams; why, in this space age and civilization, should she still be tangled in the darkness of the cobweb of superstition and ignorance, unable to see the light?

My dear sister, Ms. Shams, if you believe that non-Muslims, such as Jews, Christians, Zoroastrians, Buddhists and Bahá'ís, are unclean and infidels, then woe to the world, it is full of unclean, filthy people! How come these people, the majority of the world's population have not worried about their own filth and why haven't their scientists considered this problem?

Dear sister, Ms. Shams, thirty years after the Revolution, do you still think the same way? How long will these superstitions and prejudices continue to be handed down, from generation to generation?

I have suffered many many times; as a student I have been reprimanded and humiliated by my teachers because of my Faith. Now I have to suffer humiliation and insults from one of my own colleagues.

I remember as a child I used to go to the Ferdowsí School on Takht-i-Jamshíd Street. During my fourth year of primary school one teacher used to teach most of the subjects. One day, in the Qur'án and Sharia class, our lady teacher asked the students who were not Muslims to stand up. All the Jews, Zoroastrians, Christians, and Bahá'ís stood up. The religious minorities did not normally participate in the Islamic classes and would spend the time in the school yard.

Another Bahá'í girl and myself were standing when this venerable teacher started to insult, humiliate and vilify us. We innocently listened and only denied her calumnies. In addition, she said that the Bahá'ís disregard chastity, that sisters and brothers married and slept with each other. In a civilized country, one word of her insults would have caused her to be banned from teaching forever.

Following that day, for a long time I tried to remember which Bahá'í sisters and brothers had gotten married! I wondered whether or not there would be a day when I would wear my wedding dress and marry my brother!

I told my parents about the teacher's words. They told me that her claims were totally wrong and based on prejudice and ignorance. Bahá'ís not only avoid marrying relatives, they have in fact been encouraged to marry people from different, faraway backgrounds. The purpose is to bring the people of the world closer together and thereby contribute towards the unity of mankind and produce healthier generations.

Bahá'ís believe in the Divine origin of all religions and therefore, those Bahá'ís who were allowed to attend the Sharia and Qur'án classes were better at reading the Qur'án than others. This is because Bahá'í children are encouraged to achieve excellence in all things.

— — — — — — — — — — — — —

In the evening of the day I was dismissed from work, I discussed the matter with my family and my relatives. But that was not the end of the saga. I was sometimes invited to a government organization called the Organization of Islamic Guidance. I was interviewed by two men, one about fifty and the other a bit younger, both with short beards. They asked me a few questions about the Bahá'í Faith. It is interesting to note that they mentioned the names of the Báb and Bahá'u'lláh with due respect. They said that according to Holy Qur'án, Muhammad announced that He was the last Prophet and He called Himself the Seal of the Prophets, how could I claim that the Báb and Bahá'u'lláh are also Prophets?

I said, in the first place the followers of all religions believe that their Prophet is the last One and they await His return; they believe in special signs and events for His coming. For example, why didn't the Jews accept Christ and why didn't the Christians accept Muhammad? All the Messengers, although outwardly different, their Holy souls are animated by the same Source that appears at different times to guide mankind. In the Bahá'í Writings Muhammad has been referred to as *the refulgent lamp of supreme prophethood.*

I was again invited to the same office and more questions and answers took place. Their whole purpose was that if I returned to Islám, I could keep my job and have the rights and privileges of a Muslim citizen.

In reply I said that, as a Bahá'í, I have learned to believe in the Divine origin of all religions and I love and respect all human beings, regardless of their religion. God is One, therefore all the religions are in essence one. However, as mankind progresses, social conditions change and new social teachings become necessary; therefore, a new religion appears. The Prophets have brought suitable commandments for the time and they have spoken at the level of people's understanding when They appeared.

These replies did not satisfy their expectations. In my heart I hoped that one day those veils of fanaticism and superstition might be removed from their eyes and hearts, so that they might listen to God's new Message, based on the oneness of God, the oneness of mankind, and the oneness of religion, and act accordingly.

— — — — — — — — — — — — —

From my early youth I had a special interest in clothes design and dressmaking. I loved beautiful clothes and made unique designs for myself. After my marriage I completed a French course on fashion design at the Palace of Knowledge College and I was well-trained in this trade. After my dismissal from my job, I announced to my neighbours and friends that I was starting a dressmaking and design business at home and was available for their dressmaking requirements.

Iranian women dress very tastefully and fashionably, and custom-made dresses are very common at festivities and weddings. Ladies gradually came to me. As they were happy with my work, they introduced me to their friends and workmates. Soon I had many customers and was over-loaded. Thank God, our income rose to a level that I was able to provide for our living expenses.

About fifteen months later, in the hot summer towards the end of June 1984, the Revolutionary Guards invaded our home.

— — — — — — — — — — — —

Ghodsi Khanum, Soraya's mother

Mr. G. Fathi, Soraya's father

Soraya and Cyrus newly married in 1965

Soraya after Revolution with compulsory scarf

Ms. Fatima Fathi, Soraya's aunt

Journey through the Desert

It was a summer day late in June 1984. It was very hot and the school holidays had started. Our home was located in the Zargandeh Hills, a suburb of Tehran. It was about five o'clock in the afternoon and the neighbours had returned from work and were gathered in the alley to have a neighbourly chat, exchange the daily news and gossip, or complain about the land, the heaven and their worries.

I was wearing a sleeveless cotton dress with no collar. My head and hair were not covered and my legs were bare from the knees down. I was sitting at the sewing machine with a fan in the corner, moving the hot air around. I expected to finish the dress at hand for a client by tomorrow afternoon.

Shamim, my older son, and Basim, my younger son, together with their father Cyrus and a few neighbours were talking in the alley. Shamim entered the house excitely, passed through our short entrance hall and opened another door between the hall and the house itself.

He pushed his head through the half-opened door and with a smile said: "Mum, the Revolutionary Guards have arrived!" (Shamim would sometimes joke around and scare us by changing his voice behind the door and saying that he was a Revolutionary Guard and wanted to inspect the house!)

I quietly told him: "I have told you many times do not play this sort of joke". Shamim stopped smiling and said: "Mum, they are in our alley!"

I told him: "Go away, Shamim, let me do my work."

This time he became more serious and shouted: "Mum, go and put on your Islamic coat (a longish coat to cover the whole body), get up, hurry! They are about to enter the house!"

I accepted his words and realized that this time he was not joking, he was serious!

I immediately jumped up and put on my Islamic coat, which was hanging beside the door, and put on my scarf to cover my head. I could not find my stockings!

In the meantime, the Revolutionary Guards entered the house. They were holding a letter saying that was an order to inspect the house.

They asked me: "Are you Soraya Fathi?" I said yes, (Fathi is my maiden name). My father, Gholam Hossein Fathi, was an Army officer during the Shah's regime who had retired at his own request. I was known by that name at work.

I nervously had a brief look at the letter. It seemed to me a black sheet with mixed up words that did not mean anything to me, yet I invited them in.

In my heart I said to myself: "Assuming this warrant was a fake, who on earth had the courage to dispute it and not allow them to come in? It was impossible to argue with four armed men who were supposedly carrying out their duty."

For some time we had been hearing from people of different beliefs that this notorious group invaded their homes. For that reason we tried not to keep anything at home that would cause trouble and problems if they came for an inspection.

They knew very well that Bahá'ís never use weapons of any kind nor do they drink alcohol. We used to occasionally play cards, backgammon and chess with the children. We even threw away these games. Even those harmless games could provide a yardstick and a reason to accuse us of running a household of lust and entertainment. They could even say that we were perverse, enemies of God, and they could arrest us.

Each of these gentlemen went to a room and inspected anything and everything. The Commander of this group went to Cyrus's and my bedroom and inspected every drawer, every cabinet and every closet, messing everything up. Another guard went to the lower level and messed things up there.

The shorter, younger guard went to Shamim and Basim's room. There was a closet in that room where I kept my personal effects. These included clothes, some jewellery and a few gold coins. They were mostly gifts that, according to tradition, were given to me at my wedding and some were given to my children on the occasion of the Persian New Year's Day, called Naw Rúz. We had also stored some cash that we had been saving for a long time.

We had heard many times that the bank accounts of some Bahá'ís had been closed and their monies confiscated. Because of that, we decided to keep our savings at home as it seemed to us our home cupboard was safer than the bank.

I was standing in that room praying to God, saying: "Oh God, protect our small savings, they have dismissed us from our jobs, now they want our assets and probably our lives! Oh God, do something, do not just look down from above!"

The guard went near the cupboard, which was locked. I was standing in the corner of the room. He asked me what was in that cupboard. Quietly and calmly I told him: clothes and my personal effects, if you want I can open it. He looked at me and said: "I trust you. It is not necessary to open it." Soon after that the Commander of the group arrived and said: "Muhammad, did you inspect this cupboard?"

Muhammad said, "Yes."

He asked what was in it. Muhammad said, "Only this lady's personal effects."

In my heart I praised him and wished him God's blessings. Even now I still admire his generosity, his clear conscience, and I wish him well-being and success.

There are clean, innocent people who, because of the need for a job and daily bread, are forced to join this ignorant unjust group, but in their hearts, they are deeply upset over their cruelty and crimes; unfortunately, they have no other choice and they have to keep quiet.

Under the bed in our bedroom there was a valuable Persian rug which belonged to my aunt. My old aunt did not own anything except this rug, which she had saved for a day of need. She had gone to Rasht, a city in northern Iran near the Caspian Sea to visit my brother. To protect the rug from being stolen, she left it with us. This rug was very fine, with a very beautiful design and silk inlays. The men who were inspecting the house unfolded this rug and all of them were staring at it with their appetites growing. They quietly exchanged a few words. I told them, "This rug belongs to my aunt, who has gone to the north to see my brother and who, for safety reasons, left it in our trust."

The design on the rug was an image of the "Shah Mosque" in Isfáhán. They really wanted to take this rug together with the other things that they were taking, but I do not know what happened; they changed their minds. Maybe at first they thought that the design was based on the design of the Bahá'í buildings in Haifa, Israel! (Under the present regime anything that bears the slightest sign of Bahá'í is confiscated and destroyed). At any rate, the trouble passed and my aunt's rug with the Mosque's design was saved!

Finally, after a few hours of searching and ploughing through the whole house, they took all the Bahá'í books, family photos, and photos of Bahá'í classes, plus all the classical records that my husband had collected since he was a youth.

After they left a sigh of relief could be heard and we were able to breathe comfortably again. We all said thank God it wasn't worse! They didn't beat any of us up and they didn't arrest anyone!

It took us a while until we realized what had happened to us. Cyrus was very scared and his face had turned white. My sons Shamim and Basim were asking, what is this? What have we done wrong? Why should they attack our house? I was deeply perturbed in my heart, but outwardly I appeared calmer and more patient than the others.

Darkness had come and the neighbours left the alley to go home for dinner. Mr. Razaví, who had observed the intrusion of the Revolutionary Guards into our home from the alley, rang us late at night. He asked how we were and came over to console and comfort us. We drank tea together and calmed down a bit. Mr. Razaví was like a saviour angel who was looking after us from a distance. He said, "Cyrus-khan (in the Persian language, "khan" is a sign of respect for men), I now believe whatever you said about the harm and cruelty done to the Bahá'ís, considering that you have done nothing wrong. You are a quiet family who mind your own business. You have worked hard for so many years, why should they invade your house for no reason? Curse upon these ignorant Muslims who have deprived people of peace and comfort! If these actions are Islamic, I am no longer a Muslim! I am ashamed to call myself a Muslim."

One of the effects of this invasion by the Revolutionary Guards was that for the rest of the time we were in Tehran, my son Shamim stopped scaring us by pretending he was a Revolutionary Guard.

— — — — — — — — — — — — —

We thought that with this incident the matter had ended and we gradually returned to our daily routines. After two weeks, while we were sitting in the kitchen and having breakfast, through the kitchen window we saw a Hillman Hunter car stopped in front of our house. Two men got of the car. By their looks we could see that they were security agents. They knocked at our door and I opened it. They asked me: "Are you Soraya Fathi?" I said yes and they gave me a letter. The letter was an invitation for me to go to the notorious Evin Prison at certain time and date to be interrogated. Once again there was turmoil and agitation in the family.

Even the name of Evin caused us to tremble. People who were invited there seldom returned in one piece or even returned at all. The Evin Prison means death; it means torture, it means being held there and dying there. We did not even dare to call our friends and relations as we were afraid that they might be listening to our conversations.

The next day we went to my father's house and then to the Cyrus's mother's house and told them what had happened. They were distressed and concerned and each of them suggested a solution. But the best action for me was to go there on the day of the invitation and present myself. Why should I be afraid, what crime had I committed? In their view my only crime was that I am a Bahá'í. Okay, I am. Is my blood any more valuable than the blood of Mona, who was just only 17 years old and who sacrificed her life for her beliefs? After all, I came into this world one day and I will have to leave it another day. I am not afraid of death, but dear God, I don't know how much pain and torture I can bear! If they knew just a little bit about the Bahá'í principles and teachings, they would never harm or torture anyone.

A Persian proverb says that there is no colour darker than black. I accepted the darkest colour. I prepared myself for the worst possible treatment in the Evin Prison. They would either hold me there and finally execute me, or maybe they would let me go. I trusted God and was happy with His Will, whatever it may be.

I rushed to finish a dressmaking job I had at hand and I rang the client to come and pick up her dress. I still had some uncut fabrics from my clients. I attached labels with the clients' names and phone numbers to each one and told Cyrus that if I didn't return from the Evin Prison, to ring the clients to come pick them up.

Distressed and confused, my aunt, who had heard the story of the invasion of the so-called Guards of Justice in our house, returned from Rasht to us. Crying and cursing she said, "I will stay in this house until you came back from your interrogation at the Evin Prison. Oh God, when will You remove the hands of oppression over the heads of these wronged ones? How long shall the torment and torture continue? Where has Your justice gone?"

My aunt had lost her husband when she was young; she didn't have children and she didn't remarry. She was like a lioness, standing on her own feet until the last moment of her life. After the death of her husband, with her meagre savings she bought and sold small plots of land. Later in life, towards the end, she bought and sold other goods such as Persian carpets and gold coins, thus she was able to finance her living expenses. She (Mrs. Fatima Fathi) was always like a mother for her brothers' and sisters' children. She was very generous, kind-hearted and compassionate.

The night before the interrogation I prepared a festive dinner for the whole family with roast lamb, a traditional rice dish and a chicken casserole. After dinner we took a photo together, just in case I did not see my children again. The fact that I might not see my children again was very depressing and I would break into tears at any moment. While in my heart I was thinking of the unknown days in the Evin Prison, outwardly I seemed to be perfectly strong and calm. I was consoling my children, telling them that I would come back and that if I was kept there they should not worry; they should be happy with the Will of God, they should pray to God and beseech His support and guidance.

Mr. and Mrs. Razaví came to us for consolation and to say farewell. I was thinking, how would I feel tomorrow and who would go to the Evin Prison with me? Cyrus was so scared; he said he could not go with me. With utmost kindliness and love, Mr. Razaví said, "Cyrus-khan, don't be afraid; I will come with you."

The next day Cyrus, Mr. Razaví and I drove to the Evin Prison. Mr. Razaví was driving and at the same time giving me some advice. He told me not to be scared and not to lose my control. He said, "They might swear at you and beat you to make you angry. But you should try to remain calm and not react in anger."

I kept his advice in mind and was deeply grateful that we had such a kind-hearted, generous, true Muslim in our neighbourhood. In my heart I wished him health, happiness and continuous success. He and his wife were both like saviour angels who heard our cries and came to help us in our moments of bitter suffering. Angels do not come from the sky; look around you, you have certainly encountered a few and you will still meet more.

Metaphorically speaking, those angels have bright minds, they fly with the wings of love and affection, their pure hearts are free of prejudice and they have dedicated themselves to the service of humanity.

In the car I was immersed in my thoughts and was preparing myself for whatever might happen. I don't know how long it took to get from my home to the Evin Prison. Suddenly I heard Mr. Razavi's voice telling me that this was the entrance to the Evin Prison. I thanked him and said goodbye to Cyrus and walked towards the prison's gate. I showed my invitation to the armed guard at the gate. He sent me to a small room nearby for a security check.

I entered the room and there were two so-called Islamic sisters, they had black eyes and black eyebrows and deep voices and they had securely covered their hair. Their faces were pale and you could clearly see the hair around their lips and their chins like adolescent boys. They started to check my body and asked me to let them see inside my handbag.

In my bag I had a small towel, a tooth-brush, tooth-paste and a few paper tissues. They asked me what these were for. I told them that if I was supposed to stay there, at least I would be able to brush my teeth!

Now, after so many years have passed, remembering that event I laugh at myself and say: "If they had detained me, they would have broken my teeth just like they broke other people's teeth and I would not have needed to brush them anyway!"

After checking my body and clothes for security reasons, they blindfolded me with a piece of black cloth and told me to wait. After a moment I noticed that an official arrived, he passed me one end of a stick and told me to hold on to it while the other end was held by a man who I think was also blindfolded. They guided us to a building for the interrogation. It is kind of food for thought: the officials do not touch the Bahá'ís because they regard them as unclean; and they do not touch the Muslim victims of the opposite sex, because they regard this as forbidden. Then, how come there are so many incidents of torture in the prison? This is a riddle that perhaps the experts and specialists might be able to answer.

With difficulty, I could only see in front of my feet through the lower edge of the blindfold. After quite a while they directed us in different directions, through corridors and down some stairs. Finally we arrived in a room; they left me there and went away. I could hear the voices of officials and the cries and lamentations of some people. Amongst them there was a woman who was very afraid, crying and begging to be released.

After a few minutes I heard the voice of the interrogator, saying "Stand back!" As my eyes were blindfolded, I did not know whether he was talking to me or to someone else. This time he shouted: "Don't you hear me? Step back!" I kept going backward until I felt the wall at my back and had to stop.

I could hear the sound of the interrogator's boots pounding the ground as he walked towards me. He came very close to me and through the lower edge of my blindfold I could see his boots; I even noticed his breath on my face and could smell his sweat.

I was standing quietly, motionless. My breath was choked up and I did not know what he was going to do next. After a few moments of silence he suddenly shouted, "Concentrate properly and listen to what I am saying. In a moment I will give you some papers with a questionnaire to answer. Woe betides you if you would lie and hide the truth, do you understand?" He moved away from me and said to me, "Come here and sit down."

I released the breath I was holding in my chest and I became alive again. I could see the ground with difficulty as I slowly walked behind him. He told me, "Sit down here." I did. Somehow I noticed that he put 4-5 questionnaire forms and a pen on a chair that had an extended armrest for reading and writing.

"Do not remove the blindfold from your eyes; you are not allowed to look up," he commanded. I told him that I could not see, how was I supposed fill in the forms?

He said, "You are allowed to move your blindfold up a little, but you cannot turn your head to either side; we are observing you, lest you make a wrong move."

In my heart I addressed him saying; "O my so-called brother! If you really believe that you act with justice and truthfulness, why are you afraid of being known to others? Why don't you want to see yourself in other people's eyes? Have you ever seen yourself in your own conscience? You blindfold my eyes, do you think you can close God's eyes? Nobody should be afraid of doing the right thing."

I looked at the questionnaire. There were many questions about me, my spouse, my parents, and my sister and brothers. There were also questions about our jobs, travels, bank accounts, incomes, assets, and activities in the Bahá'í Community, as well as many others.

It probably took me about three hours to answer all the questions. It was very difficult for me to remember the exact dates of the events and activities in the Bahá'í Community. It was also difficult to remember other past matters about my family.

Nevertheless, I clearly answered all the questions with perfect sincerity and was not afraid or frightened of anyone. I called the official over and gave him the papers. I said to myself: "Have I killed anyone? Have I stolen anything? Have I committed infamy? Is being a Bahá'í a crime?"

"Being a Bahá'í is as much a sin as it is to be a Muslim or a Christian or a Jew. Following Bahá'í duties and precepts is as much a sin as it is for Muslims, Christians and Jews to follow their religious duties and precepts. I don't think that in any religion there is such emphasis on truthfulness, honesty, integrity, chastity, righteousness and love of God as there is in the Bahá'í Faith."

"Is there any colour that is darker than black? Now that I have chosen black, why should I be afraid? All right, kill me if you wish, thereby I will have peace and you will be comfortable."

A sound from the official brought me back to the present and he told me: "Wait a while. I will have a look at your papers and if there is no problem, you can go."

The time passed very slowly as I waited to get out of this so-called "fortress of justice". I could still hear the loud lamentations of the same woman begging to be released.

At last the interrogator returned and asked me to follow him to sign a paper. The paper was a sort of admittance that whatever I wrote was true and in case of a change of residence I should give them my new address.

Once again they put a stick in my hand and gave the other end to another official, and again I was guided along the same way until we reached the same room with the so-called Muslim sisters. The sisters removed my blindfold and told me: "You can go"

I ran out of the large gate of the Evin Prison like a bird leaving its cage. It was about two o'clock in the afternoon. A little further from the gate, Cyrus and Mr. Razaví were waiting for me in the car.

I went to the car and a young man was following me. Apparently he had also been interrogated. He asked me whether he could come with us to the bus stop. I said, "Sure, no problem."

We got into the car and I immediately started to relate what had happened. Mr. Razaví wisely hinted that I should leave that for later. Halfway along, the young man got out of the car and went his way. Then Mr. Razaví said:

"You should be very careful; he might be one of the prison officials."

Then I related the story of interrogation and we arrived home. My old aunt was in front of the door, sitting on the entrance steps waiting for us. As soon as she saw us she cried and said, "I have been sitting here since this morning and I have been saying prayers. You will never know how I felt. When will these people ever understand the truth and stop tormenting and oppressing the Bahá'ís? Oh God, guide them."

Shamim and Basim came to me and we embraced and thanked and praised God that we were together again. That day we celebrated.

— — — — — — — — — — — —

From the beginning of the Revolution, due to unjust pressure and cruelty towards the Bahá'ís, we had wanted to get out of the country. However, Bahá'ís were not allowed to have passports and could not leave the country. Therefore, the only solution was to escape through either the Turkish or the Pakistani borders with the help of people smugglers.

My parents and relatives were very pleased that I had returned from the interrogation in one piece. During those years and days we used to hear amazing and dreadful stories about gross mistakes and injustices in relation to sentences and investigations. In many cases they would carry out a punishment order before referring the person to the Court of law. For example, they would execute a person and later the Court would issue an order of imprisonment. Or the other way around; they would send people to prison for a certain amount of time and after the end of the prison term they would mistakenly send them to the gallows.

Many people were arrested, investigated and freed, but they would later end up in prison. For these reasons my father insisted that I should prepare myself and the family to leave the country as soon as possible.

In those days my eldest son, Shamim, was about 18 years old. Under different pretexts the authorities were capturing youth of his age and sending them to the war with Iraq. Under no circumstances would it be logical for me to let my son be taken and possibly lost in an unjust war. I firmly decided to facilitate his escape from the country.

After thinking deeply and consulting widely, I decided that it was not wise for us to flee as one group. Considering the possible dangers we might face, we could all be caught and no one would be left behind to raise the alarm or do something to rescue us. We decided to send Shamim first and make sure that he could cross the border safely; in fact, we used him as a guinea pig.

There was an old gentleman who was the intermediary between the intending escapees and the Baluchi smugglers. The Baluchis are a partly nomadic tribe who live in the Baluchistan Province of Iran. This province is located in south eastern Iran along the border with Pakistan.

This province is probably in the poorest region of Iran and has never received any special care and attention from the Government. As a result, some people of the Baluchi tribes have involved themselves in smuggling narcotics and now, during this revolutionary period, they are busy smuggling people out of their native country.

I got the telephone number of this intermediary through one of my acquaintances. I spoke to him and gave him my phone number and home address. He said that Ághá Shafí (Mr. Shafí), who was the head of a group of people smugglers, would contact me. He further said that Ághá Shafí would give me the necessary guidance. I impatiently waited for his phone call.

A few days went by and one day the phone rang. I picked up the receiver. A man with a strange accent that I had never heard before said that he wanted to speak to Soraya Khanúm. (Khanúm means Mrs. In Persian). I assumed he must be speaking on behalf of the Baluchi smugglers.

I replied, "Speaking, what news do you have?"

He said, "Khanúm-ján (dear lady), I am Ághá Shafí and I am ringing about your son. Next Wednesday I will come to your home, please have everything ready."

He immediately hung up. I quite understood what he meant. He meant that I should have the cash ready for him. For this reason I had sold my car and a few gold coins a few weeks ago and had about forty thousands toomans (the Iranian money unit), which I kept ready for him at home.

On the promised day we stayed home all day, waiting. It was mid-afternoon when the doorbell rang. A tall man with dark skin in a good-looking suit was standing there; he entered the house. I thought he was Ághá Shafí, but he said he was his cousin and his name was Haydar.

I told him that we all, that is the whole family, had decided to leave the country in three stages. First Shamim, then I with my younger son Basim, and then Cyrus would be the last one. I told him that without their help, this would be impossible.

I asked Haydar to stay for a cup of tea, but he said that he had to leave soon. I brought the cash and asked him to check it. He said that it was not necessary as he trusted me. He took the money and while walking out, he told me that Ághá Shafí would call and give his instructions.

— — — — — — — — — — — —

Three weeks passed and there was no news from Ághá Shafí. I said to myself, "That is great, they took the cash and left! So, who takes care of who? Why I was so naive that trust them? Who can ever recover that money?" It made me think of a Persian proverb that, freely translated, means that money has no power by itself; it depends upon who you give it to. If the person is honest, you get it back, if not, you lose it.

On one of the days in which I was worrying about the lost money, the phone rang. Lo and behold, it was Ághá Shafí! I became very happy and hopeful. In my heart I said to myself, "He is not one of those unscrupulous people who would betray me."

He said; "Khanúm-ján, next Monday at six o'clock in the morning catch the flight to Chahbahar. After leaving the Chahbahar airport, you will see a blue pickup truck (Ute). Get into it." Then he quickly hung up.

Chahbahar is a small town in south eastern Iran next to the Oman Sea, near the border with Pakistan.

I became agitated and stressed, Oh God what should I do? Am I doing the right thing? What could happen to my son? I would not let Shamim go alone; I would at least go with him as far as Chahbahar. Also, the officials would think that a mother and son had come to Chahbahar to buy luxury items. Being along the border, a lot of luxury items were smuggled into this town. I quickly bought two air tickets from Tehran to Chahbahar.

I packed a small travelling bag with some underwear for Shamim. I also took some food and money with me. I recommended to Shamim that if we should encounter any officials, he should be very careful about what he said. The night before the flight we went to see my parents and then Cyrus's mother. Shamim saw them for the last time before his journey, but we didn't tell them that he was about to cross the border very soon.

That night, due to worry and stress, I could not sleep. It would be a terrible day if some unforseen difficulty arose, then both of us would be imprisoned and would fall from the frying pan into the fire! We had heard plenty of bad news about the arrests of some Iranian escapees on the way to Turkey or Pakistan and we were well aware of the dire consequences. Some of them had lost their lives at the borders by either being shot, or from extreme cold or extreme thirst. In spite of all this, we risked the move and raised our hands to God, asking for His help and protection.

We got up early in the morning and Cyrus drove us to the Mehrabad Airport in Tehran. In the airport I looked around with fear and excitement; in my heart I was asking God to help us. We boarded on the plane without any hassle and after a two-hour flight we arrived in Chahbahar.

The Chahbahar airport is very small, in fact it is a military airport and under the strict control of security officials. In the airport guards were walking around and visually checking the people.

Shamim and I kept our heads down and quickly left the airport and straight away took the blue pickup truck and went into town. We got out of the truck in the town's centre, but we didn't know where to go and who to see; we started walking along the street anyway. The son of a Bahá'í friend, together with another Bahá'í youth joined us there. We knew these two young people would be Shamim's fellow travellers, but we were not sure whether they had flown or travelled by bus to Chahbahar. We later found out that they were on the same plane as us.

We were busily talking and I took this opportunity to make some recommendations to Shamim's companion, as he was a bit older than Shamim, and told them to take care of each other. In the meantime, Haydar appeared and told us to go with him to a guest house in order to rest, eat something and depart in the afternoon.

We were about to go to the guest house when a young man and two girls joined us. The father of one of the girls was also there. Perhaps, like me, he was also worried and wanted to be with his daughter until the last minute. The girls were wearing Islamic headdresses and clothes. I guess they were from the Mujahedeen group. The Mujahedeen were a religious Islamic group who politically were not in agreement with the clergy in power. Thousands of Mujahedeen were executed and imprisoned during the Revolution and many of them fled the country.

After having lunch and resting a little, we waited for Haydar in the guest house. It was very hot and uncomfortable. Finally Haydar arrived with a pickup truck and told us to get in. One of the girls and I sat in the front while the young men including Shamim and the girl with her father, sat in the rear of the truck; we then set out for Zahedan.

The heat and the burning sun on the one hand and the fear, anxiety and anguish on the other, affected me so badly that I could not bear any more travelling. As a youth I used to get severe migraines and only a sedative injection and a rest in a dark room would cure it.

But on that troublesome day I had no choice but to bear the pain and agony. Besides, I was so nauseous that I could not swallow a sedative. I wished that time would pass quickly and I would reach a safe, dark and cool place.

After two hours of travelling, the pickup truck stopped beside the road. Haydar, the driver, told me and the father of one of the girls to get out and return to Chahbahar as he was now about to reach the border. Very quickly I said good-bye to Shamim and his companions and stood on the other side of the road with the gentleman, waiting for any kind of transport to return to Chahbahar.

I immediately asked the gentleman what his name was. What would the security guards say if they saw us together? A woman with a strange man without any relationship between them, what were they doing here on a quiet road in the middle of the desert? It was therefore wise for us to get to know each other.

We quickly introduced ourselves and gave the names of our family members to each other and if it became necessary, I would tell them that I was his sister-in-law. As a pretext, I would say, "We were travelling with the family and I noticed that I had left my wedding ring in the guest house in Chahbahar and my brother-in-law is accompanying me to recover the ring; my husband, who is ill and not able to travel with me, is in Tehran".

Several cars passed and did not stop. At last a mini-bus stopped, we paid the fare and got on and returned to the same guest house. They had given my room to someone else and I was forced to rest in my companion's room.

I was moaning from the terrible headache and my face had become very pale. My companion was frightened and asked whether he should get a doctor. I told him it would not be wise to do so, hopefully I would be all right by the next morning.

I asked for some ice as one side of my head was about to explode from pain. He organised the ice, which I wrapped on my head and forehead with a cloth. I sat on the bed, which was next to a wall where I rested my head and closed my eyes.

My helpful companion went outside on the balcony, pacing back and forth and smoking cigarettes. Gradually I felt better. The next morning I had to go to the airport to return to Tehran. My companion had to do the same. We hired a taxi and went to the airport. The scheduled plane from Tehran, that was supposed to land and take passengers back to Tehran, had been high-jacked and flown to Iraq. We therefore had to wait at the airport for the next scheduled plane in the afternoon.

While our hearts were throbbing from anxiety about our children, we also had to suffer patiently waiting in the airport.

Sometimes, by coincidence, people get together and don't know its reasons. Now, after the passage of time, I realise how effective and helpful that gentleman's presence was. We were both sharing the pain of nostalgia for our children and worried about their safety. We had both suffered from unjustified accusations and subsequent cross examinations. We could understand each other's woes, troubles, and feelings, but we never spoke or complained about it.

Sometimes the pains and the pressures on individuals become a catalyst in bringing them closer to each other. In spite of the great differences in our thoughts and beliefs, we made a wise, humane friendship.

Finally, we reached Tehran on the next plane and each of us made our way home. I took a taxi. Cyrus was terribly worried and anxiously waiting. I told him that so far it had gone very well; Shamim and young people were on their way near the Pakistan border.

We went straight to Cyrus's mother and she asked about Shamim. I couldn't hold my tears back and I started crying. I told her that he was on the border between Iran and Pakistan. She couldn't believe it and I had to explain the whole adventure.

— — — — — — — — — — — — —

That night I slept very well. From the next day all my thoughts and attention were focused on the telephone, waiting for it to ring and give me news of Shamim. I wouldn't go anywhere. Even if I went to the bathroom, I would leave the door open to hear the telephone. Gradually I was becoming more impatient and distressed. Five days had already gone by and I had no news of him, I didn't know whether he was dead or alive or whether he was sick or in good health or whether he had been captured on his way to Pakistan.

My only consolation was to pray and beseech God to protect him and the other young people.

On the sixth day after my return to Tehran, the phone rang early in the morning. I jumped out of the bed and went as fast as I could to pick up the phone. It was Shamim, who told me that he was in Karachi. He and his young companions were all in good health and didn't have much trouble on their way. He added that the Baluchis were trustworthy people with integrity. I gave a sigh of relief and my mind and thoughts calmed down.

— — — — — — — — — — — — —

Earlier I had requested Haydar to contact me after delivering Shamim and his companions to the other side of the border and he had promised me that Ághá Shafí would get in touch with me.

I quickly busied myself with selling our Persian carpets, my jewellery, tables, chairs and even my personal clothes. In short, I sold what we had; the only remaining thing was our residence. We decided that after Basim and I left, Cyrus would sell the house and join us in Pakistan.

I was going through difficult, agonising days and it was no longer possible to continue with my dressmaking business. Under the pretext of a trip to the north of Iran, I did not accept any more sewing jobs and our living expenses were provided for by selling the furniture and our remaining savings.

The cash for the escape of my younger twelve years old son and me was prepared and I waited for Ághá Shafí's phone call. We prepared the necessary things for our escape.

A few weeks passed until one day the phone rang and I recognised Agha Shafi`s voice. He asked me:

"Dear lady, do you still intend to make the journey?"

I said, "Yes, definitely."

He said, "When I come to Tehran I will ring you and come to see you."

I said, "Very well", and he hung up.

From that point on I was going through difficult times, hours and days passed and I was preparing myself for a journey full of trouble and danger. With every sound of the telephone I would become excited, my heartbeat would increase and I would run to the telephone hoping to hear from Ághá Shafí.

Finally after three weeks, Agha Shafi rang, he told me that he was in Tehran and wanted to know where he could see me. I asked about his whereabouts in Tehran. He said that he was in the neighbourhood of Toopkhaneh Square.

I told him I would take the bus and meet him at bus stop number 223 and go with him to my father's home. As I had never seen him before I asked him what sort of clothes he would be wearing. He said that he would be wearing a dark striped suit and a white shirt. I told him that I was tall and thin, and I would be wearing a grey topcoat and a navy scarf and stockings.

I went to Toopkhaneh Square on a public bus and for a while I looked around for him. I walked from bus stop to bus stop and, in order to avoid the suspicions of the security guards, I would pretend that I was reading the timetables at the stops.

At the same time, from the corner of my eye I was checking the men's appearances. Because of Ághá Shafí's delay I felt uneasy and troubled in my heart. Oh God, what had happened to him? Hopefully he had not been recognised by the officials and arrested!

While my eyes were focused on a man who was coming from a distance, I suddenly heard a well-known voice from behind who said; "Khanúm-jan, is that you?"

I turned my head and looked at him. Lo and behold it was him! He was a man of medium height, with dark skin, curly hair, black eyes and a moustache. He was indeed wearing a striped suit and a white shirt. He was a real Baluchi-looking man in a European suit.

I told Ághá Shafí to accompany me, but he said he was going to buy a bus ticket. I told him it was not necessary, as I had a spare ticket. I at once put the ticket in his hand and told him to follow me. I was in the front and he was following me. Soon the right bus arrived and we got on, sat in seats in different rows and didn't speak to each other.

We got off the bus near my father's home. When we reached my father's house, I rang the bell and we both quickly entered and took the lift to the third floor.

My father and his wife welcomed us with extreme kindness and hospitality. (As a result of an illness, my mother Ghodsi Fathi, passed away and my father had remarried.)

We started talking and thanked Ághá Shafí, who had succeeded in taking Shamim and the other Iranian youth over the border. That day was a good opportunity to get to know Ághá Shafí better. He said that he spoke four languages: Persian (Farsi), Baluchi, Urdu and English. He further said that he had wives, children and houses in both the Iranian Baluchistan and in the Pakistani Baluchistan and he had Iranian and Pakistani passports.

I asked him whether he had ever been arrested. He said yes, he had even received many lashes, but by bribing different officials he managed to become free again.

Earlier I had taken the cash to my father's home. My father told Ághá Shafí, "We trust you and we will put at your disposal any amount of money you require; we ask that you take my daughter and grandchild over the border safely."

He promised to do so and if he felt any danger, he would cancel the trip. We gave him the amount of money he had requested. It was agreed that he would ring me and give me the date of departure. He also said that a family of four would be my fellow travellers. The name of the lady of that family was Parvín. Ághá Shafí said good-bye and left the house with the cash. My father said that although Ághá Shafí was involved in illegal activities in order to earn a living he appeared to be a man of good character. He further said that; "I trust that this man will keep his word and fulfil his promise."

He also said, "My dear girl, leave, go, this is not the place for you to stay. If they ask for you again, it is not likely that you will end up alive."

I returned to my home with perfect confidence that Ághá Shafí would contact me at the first, best opportunity. In the meantime, while waiting for his call, I busied myself with selling the remaining furniture and praying to God to support and protect us on this forthcoming journey.

It was towards the end of September 1984 when the phone rang, it was Ághá Shafí. He said: "Khanún-jan, next Monday catch the six a.m. morning flight to Chahbahar", and hung up.

With much anxiety, I hurried to buy two air tickets for myself and my son Basim. I was going through days of turmoil and stress. I was continually asking myself if I would be able to cross the border in a reasonably healthy condition. Would there be any difficulties? Would I ever see my son Shamim again?

We were not allowed to take many personal things with us. In the first place, the security guards could become suspicious and, secondly, in case of danger, we would have to drop everything and run away. I took a small travelling bag containing a bottle of water, a few apples, a few lemons, dates and almonds.

I made the necessary recommendations to Basim in case of encountering security guards. I told him to keep quiet and let me answer their questions. The night before our departure the phone rang and I answered with much excitement. It was Parvín.

She said that her husband had had an accident with a motorcycle rider and had been arrested and was being held at the Police Station. Therefore, they were unable to travel with us, she requested that I inform Ághá Shafí about this. This news increased my anxiety and stress. Although I didn't know this family and had never seen them before, it would have been a kind of support and encouragement to have another family travelling with us.

I at once rang my father and asked for his guidance. My father was a strong believer and a righteous man. He said, "My dear daughter, don't change your destiny because of them. It must have been God's will that they couldn't travel because of this accident. Maybe there is some blessing in this change of events. However, you should proceed with your plan and perhaps some other people will join you."

That night, due to extreme stress and excitement, I remained awake all night. That night my whole mind was occupied with the thought of what might happen tomorrow and what I could do in case of an unforseen incident.

We left the house early in the morning—three a.m.—when it was still dark and drove towards the Mehrabad Airport. While Cyrus was driving, he spoke and as usual he was against my plans for leaving the country. In this process I hardly had his cooperation or support.

Cyrus left us in the front of the airport entrance and returned home. In my Islamic topcoat and a _chador_ (a long veil that covers you from head to toe) that I had borrowed from my mother-in-law and was too short for me, I stepped into the airport. This was the second time that I wore a _chador_. The first time was when I had gone to Mashhad to see my father some years ago. The eighth Imam of Shiite Islam is buried in Mashhad and when I went to pay homage at his shrine, I had to wear a _chador_.

Since the inception of the Islamic Revolution, people's standards of belief and righteousness are being judged by their appearance. Women without any make-up, who wore _chadors_ and _burkas_, and men with messy appearances and unshaven faces are better accepted and more popular in the community. Perhaps I was also more acceptable and deserving of respect for the security officials with my ridiculous short _chador_.

Nothing happened at the airport and we boarded the plane. After one hour it was announced that, due to a possible explosive device on the plane, we would land in Bandar Abbás in order to inspect the passengers and their luggages.

I became very worried and agitated. Every delay could interfere with and overturn our travel plans and I might not arrive in Chahbahar on time to meet my fellow Baluchi travellers. If for some reason I missed my trip to Pakistan, then I was not sure of the next plan and date of departure.

Under the supervision of the officials, the passengers were guided to separate rooms for body checks. I had put some money and a few pieces of jewellery in a safety pocket that I had sown inside my trousers so that they would not be lost or stolen. Additionally, I didn't want this to be seen by the security officials, in case they saw it and asked why I needed so much money and jewellery for a short trip to Chahbahar.

I had no choice and couldn't do anything else. With fear and anxiety I went into the inspection room. After inspecting my body, the Islamic sisters asked me what was in the package sewn inside my trousers. I told them that there was some money and jewellery as I wanted to buy some material and luxury items that can be purchased in Chahbahar. Also, as there was nobody back home, I didn't want my jewellery to be stolen. That was why I was carrying it with me.

Fortunately this problem was solved and we re-boarded the plane to Chahbahar. I was constantly worrying because of our delay, God forbid that Ághá Shafí should change his plans and leave the airport! We would be obliged to return to Tehran without achieving anything.

After a few hours delay our plane arrived at the Chahbahar Airport, which was under the intense control of security guards. I looked around very carefully in the airport. It didn't seem normal; it was all very calm and quiet. There was no sign of Ághá Shafí or his cousin Haydar, or anyone else.

I became agitated and was puzzled as to what I should do. I told myself that this delay spoiled our plans and the Baluchi friends had come and gone. There were guards all around, telling people to leave the hall. (Later, when a pilot friend explained it to me, I became aware that this was a military airport. Passengers can enter the airport only at certain times, when the airplanes land and depart. Our few hours delay had actually made us untimely and unexpected arrivals.)

The passengers hurriedly rushed to the mini-bus that was waiting for them in front of the airport building and had to leave the airport's area.

We were also obliged to get on the mini-bus. The mini-bus went over a fairly long distance and passed through a large gate at the border of airport area and entered the road that leads to Chahbahar. Suddenly Basim shook me and said, "Mum, Mum, look outside! Ághá Haydar is standing there!"

Haydar was standing next to a blue pickup truck in his tribal clothes, in between several other passenger vehicles alongside the road waiting for passengers.

If Basim had not been with me, I wouldn't have recognised Haydar in his tribal clothes; he looked completely different from when I had first seen him in a normal suit!

I immediately asked the mini-bus driver to stop and let me out as I was feeling unwell. Basim and I got off the mini-bus and walked towards Haydar's vehicle. Soon after Haydar loudly announced that it cost 15 Toomans to travel to Chahbahar.

Basim and I sat in the front. The driver (Haydar) took my bag and put it in the back of the pickup truck. After travelling less than a kilometre, the vehicle stopped and a man jumped into the back of the truck and sat there.

Through the back window I was watching my travelling bag. I noticed that the new passenger opened the zipper of my bag and put his hand into it. I thought he wanted to steal something. But he withdrew his hand empty. He had probably put something into the bag. We arrived in town and a guard stopped us and asked the driver, "Who are these people?"

Haydar said these were passengers that he was taking from the airport to the guest house. Together, Haydar and the guard inspected my bag and stuck their hands into it. I couldn't see what they did. The other passenger got out and disappeared. We arrived at the guest house. Haydar told us:

"Rest here and eat something. We have to wait here until dark; I will return after sunset."

Because of our fear and anxiety, Basim and I were not able to eat anything. However, in case of thirst and extreme hunger, we were satisfied with eating some of the fruit and almonds we had carried with us.

It was gradually getting dark when Haydar returned to the guest house and told us to move quickly. Basim and I sat in the front of the pickup truck and a Baluchi man with ethnic clothes sat in the back and we travelled towards Zahedan. I don't know how many hours passed; the night had become very dark when Haydar told us that he would soon stop beside the road. He told us that we should then get out of the car and run quickly towards the desert until we disappeared from view.

At a convenient safe opportunity, when the road was totally quiet and not even a bird was flying, he stopped the vehicle. We got out of the car and he pointed in a certain direction for us to run. We immediately started to run. The driver Haydar, and the Baluchi man made a U-turn and swiftly returned in the direction of Chahbahar. While I was holding Basim's hand and running breathlessly, I was thinking in my heart, "Had they planned to harm us? Maybe they left us here to be torn apart by the wolves, oh God, help us!"

With all our strength we continued to run over sand, gravel and rocks. We climbed a small hill and walked down the other side. Down there, three armed Baluchis with three donkeys were waiting for us.

It was a very dark night, as if the moon and the stars had gone on strike and gone elsewhere. I could hardly see the faces of these companions. I only could see their white teeth, their eyes and the strap wrapped around their head. I instantly asked them:

"Where is Ághá Shafí. Where are the others?"

They replied, "Ághá Shafí is waiting for you at the Pakistan border. The family that were supposed to go with you couldn't travel because of a car accident. We had planned to travel with a car, but due to our small number we are taking a different route."

I had no other choice but to continue with the journey; there was no return for me.

I had to put my destiny in the hands of these men whom I didn't know and had never seen before. And, in this desert without water and even a blade of grass, I had to go forward on my own with only my twelve years old son. I told myself that any harm and pain that might afflict me in this desolate area would not be any worse than the torments and tortures in the Evin Prison.

I reminded myself of what my father had said, "Don't be afraid of anything, rely upon God, he will support and protect you."

The men told us to mount the donkeys. I had never in my life ridden a donkey, but in this situation I had to do it. Basim sat on another donkey. The other three men walked, and when they were tired they would mount the third donkey, which was carrying a load of bits and pieces. After about three hours we stopped somewhere and sat on the ground. We ate dates and dry bread. The men spread a blanket on the ground and said I could lie down to rest. I told them that I was all right and that I would sit on the ground.

From the lack of sleep I had no more strength and resistance, nevertheless I kept my eyes open for the hope of the morning light and sunrise; I was thinking about my unknown future destiny.

After a short rest we mounted the donkeys again and continued on our way. Sitting on a donkey's back is very hard for those who are not used to it. For that reason I started to feel sores on the side of my legs. I gradually got used to the darkness of the night in the heart of the desert and I no longer suffered from missing the stars.

The sound of the puffing of my companions as they climbed the slopes, together with the sound of the crushing of dry bushes under their feet and the sound of donkeys grinding grass provided a heart-soothing sound in the middle of the desert.

Basim was riding in front and had fallen asleep. He almost fell off the back of the donkey. I shouted at once: "Basim, be careful! Don't fall!"

The head of the group quietly came close to me and whispered, "Khanúm, don't speak in the desert, the sound spreads far and wide and they will notice that we are here."

That night we kept moving until the morning.

Gradually the early morning light overwhelmed the darkness of the night and the beautiful sun displayed itself with its loving affection, creating magnificent, incomparable picturesque scenery.

In the daylight I could see the sun-burnt faces of my companions. They, just like Ághá Shafí, seemed to be simple and trustworthy. The oldest of them, whose name was Omar, was about 50, the other two perhaps 35 and 40 years old.

We stopped to rest and have a cup of tea. Basim collected scrubs and twigs from the desert. Soon a fire was lit and they boiled water in an old smoky kettle and dropped tea leaves into it. Tea was ready! They had a few tin cups, some dry bread, and some dates with them, and I had a few apples. These were the ingredients of our breakfast. Although I never had a cup of tea and food like this and I would always emphasize cleanliness and hygiene, I drank the tea due to my extreme tiredness and thirst. It was so tasty, as if it was a cup of tea from heaven and its water was from the river of paradise, its taste was sweeter than the sweetness of honey!

After a short rest we started to move again. As the day progressed, the weather became hotter and we became thirstier. Basim and I finished the little water we had. Now we only had a few apples and lemons to quench our thirst.

The sound of guns in the surrounding mountains made us anxious and afraid. I asked Omar what was happening. He said, "Khanúm don't worry, there are security guards around here and they are afraid of us Baluchis, therefore they shoot into the air in order to chase us away from this area."

I said, "Fine, but what would you do if they came close?"

He said, "They wouldn't dare come close, but if they got involved in a fight with us, we would skin them alive with these daggers!"

In my heart I praised the manliness and the courage of these Baluchi men. They face an enemy like a blood-thirsty lion, while protecting a helpless female with humility and respect.

We continued on our way. In the daylight I was able to see the desert more properly. As far as the eyes could see there was sand, rocks, dust and occasionally, shrubs and bushes. I could hardly see any green bushes. In some areas a few reasonably high hills were visible.

It was very interesting to observe that the donkeys were walking in the front and the Baluchis behind them. I asked Omar, "How come the donkeys know their way so well?"

He replied, "First of all, donkeys are very smart and, secondly, we previously drove a jenny (a female donkey) along this route and these donkeys follow the same route using their sense of smell." (It is very interesting to note that amongst animals, the females play an important role. They go in front and guide the male animals along the right path. I imagine that female donkeys have achieved higher rights even without the help of Animal Rights Organizations!).

Omar and his mates knew the desert like the palm of their hands. Even though there were no obvious direction signs, every rock, hollow depression or elevation would indicate the route of their journey. Often in places where they would stop we could see some rubbish that had been left behind, such as empty food tins, chocolate and biscuit wrappers. It was as an indication that there was a lot of trafficking of people who fled the country and stopped at these places for a rest.

It was gradually getting dark again when we were climbing up a high hill to go down its other side. Omar told us to get off the donkeys and walk up the hill. As a result of the lack of sleep I was extremely tired and exhausted, and I was walking and breathing hard and fast. One of the Baluchis held my hand and said, "Let me help you." With his help, the climb became easier. Soon after my hand started to burn from the heat of his hand and I pulled my hand away and told him that I could manage by myself.

It was midnight and we were all very tired. Basim and I lay down beside each other to one side. I was almost dying from the pressure of sleeplessness and fatigue. I was longing for a bit of sleep, but I knew that if I shut my eyes I would unconsciously fall into a deep sleep. I forced myself to keep my eyes open in order to observe what was happening around me, while saying prayers in my heart.

Each of my companions was lying down and silence had covered the desert's atmosphere. Suddenly, the heehaw of one of the donkeys broke the silence. He was braying so loud that his noise could be heard from miles away. One of the Baluchis got up and I am not sure what he did, but after a while he managed to silence the donkey. I was told that the donkey had been calling for a jenny. Perhaps the donkey had been calling to the same freedom-loving jenny that went in this direction before!

Early in the morning we started moving. Drinking water vanished and I was very thirsty. The fact that I knew that there was no more drinking water made me thirstier. After a while we reached a low-lying point surrounded by some hills. In a corner, there was a puddle with some muddy water.

My companions filled up the kettle at once, boiled the water and made some tea. I had a lemon or two. I squeezed the juice into my tea and it helped to somewhat quench my thirst.

It was astonishing to note that Omar and his mates did not feel any fatigue, thirst or hunger. Just like camels, they could tramp the desert and never complain about the lack of water. They would constantly smoke and that was their only pleasure.

After a short rest we continued on our way. Towards midday the weather became hotter and hotter. The thirst was unbearable. Basim was very patient and did not complain in spite of all the difficulties. My lips were dried and cracked because of the thirst and heat. I was willing to pay a thousand Toomans in order to drink a glass of cool water.

Is there anything more enjoyable than a sip of water? Why didn't I realize how valuable it was? I blamed myself for hosing down and washing the tiles in my yard so many times with that valuable water. Woe to me, how could I savagely and liberally waste this bounty of God? I wished that there was a drop of that clean water here! The thirst, on the one hand, and the pain of the sores on my legs caused by the friction with the donkey's saddle, on the other, were causing me enormous discomfort. I had no choice but to suffer and endure; in any case, I was hopeful that there would finally be a solution for all my problems and a remedy for all my pains.

After a while we arrived at a water puddle, the donkeys rushed to the puddle, drank from it, and then peed into it. We didn't drink from that water and we continued on our way.

Near sunset we arrived at a wide, shallow river with flowing muddy water. Omar said: "<u>Kh</u>anúm, this river is the border between Iran and Pakistan, once we cross this river we are in Pakistan and there will be no danger and nobody can touch us."

With joy and a smile I said: "Is that true? Oh God, I can't believe it!" I didn't know whether to cry or to laugh. I felt happy because I was finally being freed from so much cruelty and the injustice of the authorities, and on the other hand, I was deeply sad because why should I be forced to leave my home country? Why should I have to leave the motherland in which I had grown up? The pain I was feeling was as bad as losing my mother. Yes, Iran was my mother, my love, my memories, my life, my existence, my soul and my spirit. *Iran was my home. Iran is no longer my home; an unsafe home is nothing but a prison.*

We crossed the river on the back of the donkeys and got down on the other side. We washed our hands and faces and, due to our enormous thirst, we drank the muddy, brackish river water.

I turned around, threw a last look at the other side and said farewell to my dear motherland. I beseeched God's blessings for her and wished her freedom and safety.

— — — — — — — — — — — —

top left and right, Baluchi woman and man in their ethnic clothes
bottom, Desert in Baluchistan

Soraya with Agha Shafi's scarf and borrowed hair on the roof in Peshawar

A bakery in Peshawar, Basim standing on the right and Shamim sitting on the left side

One of the National Festivals in Islamabad

On Pakistan Soil,
Seeking Refuge in Australia

We were now in Pakistan, on the border of a large plain; it was getting close to sunset. The sun was setting with great dignity. Omar said, "Khanúm, we should see Ághá Shafí very soon." I became very happy to hear that, as I had special trust in Ághá Shafí.

While I was looking around and enjoying the beautiful colours appearing in the sky and on the plain, I noticed a beacon of light that was moving from one side to another. Then I saw that Omar had a mirror in his hand and was using the reflection of the sun, transmit signals to the other side and receive signals from them. Signals were sent and received several times and then we continued on our way.

After a short time Omar told us that we would wait for Ághá Shafí right here. A few minutes later I noticed a pickup truck in the distance, coming towards us. The truck was raising a lot of dust behind it. For a few minutes the beautiful painting of the land and the horizon, with its diverse colours, became invisible beneath the cloud of dust.

The vehicle stopped in front of us and with glory and dignity, Ághá Shafi got out of the truck in his ethnic clothes and white head cover like a prince from a fairy tale.

After mutually saying hello and how are you? he asked me, "Khanúm-jan, how was your trip? I hope you didn't suffer."

I said: "Oh, the trip was not bad; it was fairly good, I couldn't expect more."

He asked: "Were you harmed on the journey? Are you satisfied with these men?"

This time I understood what he meant. I said:

"I had no annoyances on the journey and my companions were very honest and trustworthy. I was happy with them."

Then Ághá Shafí talked to them in the Baluchi language and took some of the load from one of the donkeys, he took some cash from his vehicle and divided it between the three Baluchis. And then he sent them back. I was told that they would return to the Iranian part of Baluchistan together with their donkeys.

Ághá Shafí went back to the vehicle and brought a large bag that contained ethnic clothes. He gave one set of ethnic clothes to Basim to wear and he also gave me a set of the same. He told me: "Khanúm-jan, please wear these on top of your clothes."

Then he walked to his vehicle and took out a large blue silk scarf with yellow and red flowers that seemed to be three dimensional.

I was very tired and I was sitting on the ground, he came to me and unfolded the scarf and threw it over my head and face and said: "Khanúm-jan, always keep your face covered so that nobody can recognise you, because from now on wherever we go I will introduce you as my wife and Basim as my son, and remember not to speak a word because your accent indicates that you are a stranger here.".

While I was sitting on the ground, I looked at him from under the silk scarf. For a moment he appeared like a god on earth, a prince from a fairy tale who reigns over the desert. Now he was my protector and guard, he was the one with whom I would complete the rest of the journey without any danger. I was so tired and thirsty and I had suffered so much on the way, that I wanted to tell him to sit beside me for a while, let me rest my head on his shoulder because I needed a safe place to rest. I was dying for a bit of sleep, I was thirsty for a sip of clean water, I was slowly dying, I had no more energy to move.

I became aware of myself and said, "All right, Ághá Shafí, I will cover myself and I will not speak to anyone."

We got into the truck as it was getting dark. He drove the truck at high speed with the lights switched off, veering from left to right like a wild deer due to the rough ground. In the distance I noticed lights flickering.

I said: "It looks like we are coming closer and closer to a village."

He said: "Yes, there is a small village in which we will rest for a few hours."

As we got nearer to the village, the sound of Indian melodies in the air enlightened my spirit. The sound of music gave me vitality and took away my fatigue. During the past few years I couldn't listen to music because, in the view of the Islamic fundamentalists, it was illegal because it was the cause of immorality and perversity.

We arrived at a hamlet with small houses built beside each other. We accidentally met a few people to whom Ághá Shafí spoke in Baluchi. Soon he opened a locked house and asked Basim and me to enter. He told us: "Lock the door from the inside and do not open it to anyone." He went to get some dinner for us.

It didn't take long before he returned with a tray of warm food and drinking water.

He told us to eat dinner and rest as we had to leave in a few hours. In the house there was a moderately large room. In one corner there was a toilet and a barrel of water and a watering can beside it. Basim and I ate our dinner. I don't know what it was, but as we were very hungry and thirsty, we enjoyed the food very much. As we were immensely tired, we lay down on a bed in the room and slept like the dead.

At the sound of a knock on the door, I jumped up from my sleep and woke Basim, who was in a deep sleep, telling him that we had to leave at once. When I opened the door, I saw Ághá Shafí and one of his mates waiting for us. We got into the truck. Basim and I sat in the front and the Baluchi man sat in the back. We again drove through the desert in the middle of the night, without a road, no lights, no life, and no birds flying around.

After half an hour Ághá Shafí said that the truck tires had been punctured and he kindly asked us to get out so that they could change the tires. He spread out a blanket at distance from the truck and told us to rest while they fixed the truck.

Basim and I lay down alongside each other, away from where the truck was parked. I was curiously observing them to see what they were doing. They took off many parts of the truck such as seats, doors and tires, and then, they put them back. I never understood what the connection was between the punctured tires, the seats and the doors of the truck!

I am not sure whether they placed something somewhere in the truck or they took something out of the body of it. Afterwards I noticed that they sat beside a brazier with glowing charcoal. From the scent that filled the air it was obvious that they were smoking opium.

In my childhood we used to live on a street called Karaj Boulevard and Mr. Yazdí used to live with his young wife and children a couple of houses away from us. Mr. Yazdí was much older than his wife and he was one of the wealthy bazaar merchants.

(A bazaar is a kind of business and trading centre in Iran and other Middle Eastern countries.)

Mr. Yazdí and his family had a cook, a gardener, and a driver at their disposal. In those days in the summer we used to sleep in the yard under mosquito nets. Late at night a special scent would fill the air in our yard from Mr. Yazdí's garden. My grandmother used to tell us that Mr. Yazdí had set up his brazier and *bafoor* (a special pipe for smoking opium). In those days I became familiar with the scent of opium smoke.

Ághá Shafí called out, saying, "Khanúm-jan get up, the truck is fixed!"

We got into the truck and Ághá Shafí's Baluchi mate got out near a village while we kept on going. Ághá Shafí, just like a jockey in a horse race who lashes his horse to run faster, accelerated the truck to top speed. I am not sure whether he was awake or asleep. It seemed to me that he was in another world, but he knew the route by heart. For him it made no difference whether it was day or night.

I was sitting beside him in the truck in the middle of night and suffering from what I had witnessed. I was worried about my unknown destiny. I was not sure where I was going and I was thinking about the darkness of tomorrow. The smell of opium was coming from Ághá Shafí's breath and body and it had filled up the entire space in the truck. I was turning my face to the side window to separate myself from his small world.

The breeze of the fields and the desert with its delightful fragrance was soothing my face and calming me down. It sang into my ears that, as long as there was beauty and tenderness in the fields and the plains, there would also be a bright tomorrow.

Like a hero in the movies, Ághá Shafí was skilfully driving the truck forward. He drove according to a previously designed time and plan without any mistakes. I was amazed by what I had seen from these people over the last few days! Did they imitate Hollywood films or did the film-makers learn from them? I don't know; whatever the case may be, perhaps these men did not play roles, this was their real life. And I, without any previous knowledge and experience, had to be with them unwillingly in order to see the real story of a real life, rather than watching it in a Hollywood movie. This was the real life of some fellow Baluchi citizens. In any event, I was only a tiny part of the people being driven from one place to another and in that reality I was a spectator rather than a player.

— — — — — — — — — — — — — —

Gradually it became brighter and Ághá Shafí was getting down from his high caused by his earlier smoking of opium. We arrived at a village where the dwellers were still sleeping and it was quiet everywhere. Basim and I were led to a room, locked in and had to wait for the next order for action. I, for one, had no strength due to exhaustion and lack of sleep. I just dropped on the floor in the room and my eyes closed of their own will.

The sun was shining brightly when the door opened and Ághá Shafí entered, bringing a tray of breakfast goodies.

He said: "Khanúm-jan, today we shall fly to Karachi. Unfortunately there were only two seats. Today you and I will fly and Basim, together with my brother-in-law, will join us tomorrow." Basim, in his childish world said, "Fine, Ághá Shafí, I will fly tomorrow".

Suddenly I was shocked from an intense fear of what might happen and I was close to fainting and falling to the ground. That moment was the most frightening moment in my whole life, for I was reminded of a dreadful report I had read in one of the Tehran newspapers:

"A woman was travelling by bus on one of the country roads of the Province of Khorasan, holding a baby on her chest, under her *chador*. The other passengers noticed that the baby neither cried nor ate anything. They became suspicious of the woman and reported their suspicions to the officials. The officials checked the woman and found that the baby was dead and narcotics had been placed in its stomach."

I thought in my heart that they might do the same to my child, or they might have other evil intentions in their heads. I threw an angry look at Basim and told Ághá Shafí: "No way, we go to Karachi together, I will not be separated from my child and I will wait until tomorrow."

I felt anguished and frighted in my heart as I never had before. With every moment that passed I was losing more and more of my trust in Ághá Shafí. If he separated me from my child, what could I do? In my heart I immediately raised my hands to God and asked for His assistance and protection.

He left and returned after two hours. He said: "Khanúm-jan, I have good news for you. A passenger cancelled his flight and we now have three tickets."

Upon hearing this good news, the light of hope dawned in my heart and I was revived again. He further added: "I told them that you are my wife and that Basim is my son, remember to cover your face."

Dressed in our ethnic Baluchi clothes, Basim, Ághá Shafí, myself and a Baluchi man got into the car. Ághá Shafí was carrying a briefcase with him. We travelled towards a small town near the border and from there to a flat field. This was apparently a private airport and from there we flew to Karachi in a small airplane.

The airplane was a small, light one and had room for only seven people, including the pilot. The wind was pushing the plane from one side to another and I was expecting that it would crash at any minute.

After more than one hour of fearful flight we arrived at the Karachi airport. We walked to the airport hall from the tarmac and from there to the exit door and onto the street.

When I saw the people and the streets I was sure that I was really in Pakistan and no longer in danger. I breathed comfortably and thanked God in my heart. We entered the street and saw crowds moving in different directions; the weather was fairly warm. The noise of cars and their horns, and the hustle and bustle of the crowds were an indication of a highly populated city. There were a great number of taxies and other cars for hire in rows beside the footpath and they were asking us to get into their vehicles. But Ághá Shafí's eyes were moving around, looking for a different taxi.

After a few minutes he pointed to a taxi that was approaching. The taxi arrived and we put our meagre luggage in the boot and got into the car. On the way I noticed that the driver of this taxi must be one of Ághá Shafí's workers. They spoke in Baluchi and from the way they had greeted each other you could see that they were not strangers.

After passing through noisy, crowded, polluted streets, we stopped in front of a hotel and got out of the car. That quarter of the city was extremely crowded and people were almost walking on each others toes.

Basim and I picked up our bags, but Ághá Shafí left his briefcase in the taxi and let the driver take it with him. We entered the hotel and went up to the third flour. Ághá Shafí let us into one of the rooms and told us: "Rest here and make absolutely sure that you don't open the door to anyone because there are swindlers and criminals trafficking here. I am going to bring you some food."

We washed and refreshed ourselves in the hotel's bathroom, which only had cold water. Ághá Shafí soon returned with a tray of food and drinking water. I asked him whether there was a pharmacy nearby. He said to me: "Whatever you want, I can get for you. It is not at all wise for you go out."

I asked him to buy some disinfectant and penicillin powder to treat the sores on the back of my legs. He went out and returned very soon with the medicines I had requested. I thanked him for successfully having brought us to Karachi and told him that it was now time for me to call a taxi and go to the Bahá'í Centre in Karachi.

Ághá Shafí became concerned and said: "No, Khanúm, you don't know the way; in addition to that, if you were caught by the police you would be in trouble because you don't have a passport. Wait a little longer and I will take you to the Bahá'í Centre myself. Do you have any Rupees (Pakistani currency) with you?"

I said: "No, I am glad you mentioned it. I have sufficient Iranian currency. Would you be able to exchange them for Rupees?"

He said, yes, he could. I immediately gave him all my Iranian money and he gave me Rupees in accordance to the market value at that time.

After a short while we took a taxi to the Bahá'í Centre. On the way we went through nicer, quieter parts of Karachi. We passed through a beautiful street near the water and could see the sea. We then passed through a street with many trees and after a while we arrived at a white building. Over the building's front door was written: Bahá'í Centre. I thanked God in my heart that we had finally arrived at our destination.

We got out of the taxi and Ághá Shafí accompanied us to the office, which was located on the second floor. We entered the office and a lady named Mrs. Khoshnoudi lovingly welcomed us. I told her that I was a Bahá'í and that I had arrived today after a few days journey. Mrs. Khoshnoudi asked us to sit down; she wanted to ask us a few more questions. In the meantime Ághá Shafí appeared to be satisfied as he realised that I was in a safe place and the people here would take care of Basim and me. He said:

"Khanúm-jan, I have to go, the taxi is waiting for me." I thanked him sincerely and wished him all the best under God's protection.

At that moment I felt like a child who is holding her mother's hand on the first day of the school and doesn't want to let her go because she is afraid of being separated from her mother. I felt the same with Ághá Shafí, I had gotten used to him. He was a brave man with a fighting spirit who could overcome difficulties and remove obstacles. He was like a rescuing angel who saved my son from being signed up and taken to the war with Iraq and the one who also rescued me from probable danger in the future. He had saved us from Tehran, whose sky was overcast with the clouds of fear and injustice. Step by step he was our guardian and our protector along this dangerous journey. I was choked up and had tears in my eyes. I followed him up to the head of the stairs and followed him with my eyes to the exit gate in the garden. I knew I would never see him again. I suddenly called out loudly to him, saying: "Ághá Shafí, don't forget to also bring Cyrus out." He replied that he would contact him.

I returned to the office and continued talking with Mrs. Khoshnoudi. She asked me a number of questions. It was agreed that I would arrange through my relatives back in Iran to send my credentials to her office as a registered Bahá'í.

In the Bahá'í Faith individuals have no authority and there are no religious positions such as priests, mullahs, muftis, pastors, or rabbis. The social, administrative and spiritual affairs are managed and administered by elected bodies. These bodies, such as the Local Spiritual Assembly, are elected by the local community, while the National Spiritual Assembly is elected by delegates from the local communities.

The members of these Assemblies are elected by a majority vote of the Bahá'ís. For this reason, the names of the Bahá'ís must be registered for the election statistics so no one could claim to be a Bahá'í unless he or she was registered. Therefore, it was essential that I should produce evidence that I was a Bahá'í.

The Bahá'í Centre of Karachi, which was adorned and beautified with green trees and beautiful flowers, provided a pleasant, calming environment. Now I was sure that I was in a safe place and from now on, with God's confirmation, I was under the protection of the National Spiritual Assembly of the Bahá'ís of Pakistan.

There was a large number of recently arrived refugees in the Pakistan Bahá'í Centre and almost all the rooms were occupied. A few other women and I were located in one of the rooms. They gave us a few blankets and we slept on the floor. I folded the _chador_ I had brought with me from Iran and used it for a pillow under my head. That night, for the first time after five days of wandering, I slept comfortably, without any troubles in my mind.

The next day Mrs. Khoshnoudi sent me and a few others to Lahore. We stayed one night in a Bahá'í friend's home there and the next day we travelled to Peshawar, where my other son, Shamim, was staying as a refugee.

We got on a mini-bus going in the direction of Peshawar. The driver of the mini-bus drove better and more carefully than Ághá Shafí. But, like other Pakistani drivers, he ignored his brake pedal and accelerated instead, honking his horn and speeding along the bitumen and dirt roads.

It took us more than half a day before we arrived in Peshawar. Peshawar is a small town located on the border with Afghanistan. There were many refugees from Afghanistan who spoke Farsi (Persian). Most of them were in the bakery, butchery and green grocery business.

The people of Pakistan were generally very friendly and hospitable, and most of them were familiar with the English language, hence we could communicate with them in our broken English.

As soon as we arrived in Peshawar, Basim and I went to a shop owned by a Bahá'í friend and with his help I got Shamim's address. Basim and I hired a rickshaw (a kind of three-wheeled transport) and went in the direction of his address. We got out of the rickshaw at the head of a narrow alley. There was a ditch down the middle of this alley with running water that was carrying sewage and spreading an unpleasant smell in the air.

We accidentally met two Iranian Bahá'í youth and asked them about Shamim's whereabouts. Since the day Shamim left Iran for Pakistan our only communication was by telephone. With great difficulty he would call us via Pakistan's telephone and telegraph office. We only had three telephone communications with him and that was with great care and caution. We also couldn't inform him about our travel plans because Ághá Shafí would contact us about it at the last minute. The youth told us to follow them as they lived with him in the same house. The youth entered the house and told Shamim that there were some people waiting to see him.

Shamim, who didn't know that we were coming, was overjoyed and excited to see us.

After about two months of separation we were reunited and our hearts were enlightened. It was a sweet, unforgettable moment. The love of seeing my son in good health made me cry from joy and happiness.

That night we had an elaborate dinner cooked by the boys. It was very delicious. Their house was in very good order and, like a small barrack each one had a duty to perform. A few days passed until, with the participation of two other families, we rented an apartment. This was a three-bedroom apartment on the second floor on Arbab Road. One room was assigned to me and my sons, Shamim and Basim. Another room was assigned to four young girl students, and the largest was assigned to the Afsharí family, who had three beautiful, intelligent children.

The girls, like thousands of other Bahá'í students, were deprived of tertiary education. They had been trying to escape from the country one way or another and arrive in a free country where they could receive a higher education.

One of those girls had beautiful long hair that reached her waist. One day while we were hanging out the washing on the line and Shamim was taking photos, I asked the girl to lend me her hair for a moment. She hid herself behind me, out of the camera's view. She spread her hair over my shoulders and chest and Shamim took a photo at this instant. For weeks this photo was the cause of laughter and amusement for us.

It was not easy for 12 people to live in a small apartment which had no bath and no hot water, and there were other difficulties. For example, I remember that every morning we had to queue for the toilet. The kitchen was being used for both cooking and washing. To wash our clothes and our bodies we had to warm the water up and pour it into a large container before we could use it.

Our life was very primitive and simple. At night we would sleep on grass matts. For a little more comfort, the residents of the apartment consulted with each other and decided to use the kitchen in turns. We eventually agreed to use the kitchen for cooking and preparing food in the morning and in the afternoon for personal cleaning and washing clothes.

We consulted together because we were following one of the important Bahá'í teachings, which is consultation. (Consultation on social and personal matters is very important in the Bahá'í Faith. This means respect and consideration is given to the views and the suggestions of the community members on the basis of equal rights for every one. A decision is usually taken by a majority vote after discussing an issue.)

Despite all the difficulties and discomfort, Shamim and Basim were very patient, they never complained or nagged. Perhaps bearing difficulties would be useful and necessary for them to become hard-working, industrious men in the future. At any rate, their trouble and experience with life in Pakistan was more useful to them than joining the army.

Back in Tehran most of us were used to having large, well equipped and relatively comfortable houses and naturally it was very hard for us to bear these frugal conditions.

Most of us had become very sensitive and irritable, but at last we concluded that we had no other choice except to be patient and practice self-restraint. Problems could be solved by mutual love and consideration to keep things in good order and make the necessary arrangements.

Most days we would eat simple foods because the meat that was available at the butcher shops were not hygienic. Our food consisted of potatoes, eggs, bread, yoghurt and legumes, like peas and lentils.

Sometimes we would take our cooked meals to the room of the Afsharí family. There we would spread a large tablecloth on the floor and place the food on it and we all would enjoy it together. After the meal we had the luxury of drinking tea, eating sweets and fruits. Sometimes we would listen to Iranian or Indian music, dance and tap our feet.

Fortunately the Spiritual Assembly of the Bahá'ís of Peshawar would regularly arrange spiritual programs and prayer meetings which would uplift and strengthen our souls and console our pains and worries.

In the first few days we contacted the United Nations High Commission for Refugees (UNHCR) in order to obtain ID cards so that, in case of need, we could identify ourselves.

Each refugee that was recognised as such received a small amount of money from this organization. This pay was hardly enough to cover all the expenses. Therefore, we were forced to live with the greatest economy and be content. Living under the same roof in a large group was one of the ways to reduce expenses.

Soon we obtained application forms from the office of the United Nations Organization. In those days I had a sister living in Canada and a brother in America, but I preferred to move to Australia because I had a special liking for Australia and its unique species of animals.

Australia and its environs were already in my childhood dreams and gradually occupied parts of my thoughts and existence. Australia was my goal and my wish was to get there.

During my childhood my father used to call me his "Australian girl". He used to pat my shoulders and tell me, "You are my Australian girl".

With these words he meant that I, just like Australia, was unique and exceptional.

In the same manner he would call my older brother his Austrian boy and my younger brother, who had fair skin and hair, his American boy.

It is very interesting to note that my older brother went to study in Austria and my younger brother went to America. And, after going through difficult adventures, I reached Australia, which was the adored place of my desires and wishes.

— — — — — — — — — — — —

With the help of a Bahá'í youth whose English was good we filled in the application forms for Immigration and sent them to the Australian Embassy in Islamabad. It had been about three years since my older brother had migrated to Australia and he had sponsored us for the required expenses. Our moments of anguish and waiting had started and we counted the days in anticipation of any kind of reply from the Australian Embassy.

One of our sweetest moments would be the arrival of a letter from the Embassy so that we knew where we stood and what our next move should be. Oh, how beautiful, sweet, and bitter is waiting!

Bahá'í friends whose visa or travel tickets had arrived would celebrate by offering sweets to other refugees. And when leaving they would hand over their belongings, such as bedding and kitchen utensils, to the new arrivals and tears of joy would run down their faces.

After several letters to the Embassy, we finally received a reply asking us to go Islamabad for our medical checkups.

It was about this time that Cyrus, in the company of some other friends, arrived in Pakistan and joined us. He had managed to sell our only possession, the house we had in Tehran, and was able to exchange the proceeds and transfer them out of the country through a trustworthy person. Unfortunately, as the value of the Iranian currency had continually gone down we only received a comparatively small amount. It should also be mentioned that when Cyrus was dismissed from the oil company, he lost all of his superannuation and never got anything back.

We quickly prepared ourselves for our medical examinations and travelled to Islamabad. The doctors were selected by Embassy.

Islamabad was a very clean and beautiful city. The buildings, the surrounding parks and the gardens with beautiful flowers and shrubs were infinitely interesting and praiseworthy. Islamabad was like a gem in Pakistan's crown that had been polished with great care and tenderness.

In Islamabad we could forget that we were in Pakistan as there was a different impression with a different atmosphere, one with a peaceful feeling. It took some time until we were informed of the results of our medical examinations, which were all good and acceptable. The following procedures were an interview, the issuance of our visa, and the date of our flight to Australia. Now our thoughts and talks were focused on our departure.

I deeply wished that the days and weeks would pass very quickly and we would soon be rescued from this unsettled, distressful situation. My heart was longing for a cosy, quiet, clean room away from noise and traffic. I was asking God:

Will I once again be able to be in the privacy of my own room?

Will I once again be able to prepare and cook food in my own kitchen?

Will I once again be able to stand under a warm shower and wash my body?

Will I once again be able to use toilet in my own house?

Oh God! Do You hear my earnest requests and will You answer my pleadings positively?

The bitter moments of waiting were passing at the speed of a snail. In hopes of a sweet tomorrow, I absorbed the bitterness of today. In hopes of a bright tomorrow, I arose from my sleep and looked forward to other tomorrows. The thoughts of being freed from the cage made me feel alive again.

After some time we were invited by the Australian Embassy to Islamabad for an interview. The day before the interview we washed ourselves in our multipurpose kitchen and in the morning we put on our best clothes and travelled to Islamabad by mini-bus. We arrived at the designated office on time.

Cyrus had studied in England for a few years and was familiar with the English language. He was able to answer the questions and the rest of us could introduce ourselves in our broken English. After about 20 minutes we left the office and returned to Peshawar.

Thereafter we were very hopeful that everything would be all right. We impatiently waited for the Embassy's reply and our travel visas. It took about two months until one day we were informed that some registered mail had come for us from the Embassy.

For security reasons the letters usually went to the post office box of the Spiritual Assembly of the Bahá'ís of Peshawar and from there they were passed on to the recipients. With joy and enthusiasm we opened the letter and it was a great joy to see that the visa had arrived and the date of departure was announced. We cried from joy and, to be sure of what we had read, we read the letter again several times. We immediately informed our friends and housemates and celebrated the good news by providing sweets for the friends.

The happy days had come. As they say in Persian, we couldn't fit into our skins from joy. We were counting every minute in expectation of departing from Pakistan. For almost nine months we had suffered in anticipation of leaving Pakistan. We gave our meagre things to other families and we bought a few Pakistani handicrafts as souvenirs in memory of our days and months in Pakistan.

Our flight left from Islamabad and, after stopovers in Karachi and Singapore, we arrived in Brisbane on 26th June 1985. Brisbane is the capital of Queensland in Australia.

My brother and his wife had come to the airport to welcome us. After many years of separation we were overjoyed to see each other. They took us to their town of residence on the Gold Coast. Along the way I was staring at the landscape and was stunned by seeing so much beauty and such a peaceful scenery.

Their residence was in an apartment overlooking the water. The beautiful surrounding views and the blue ocean opened a little window of paradise for us. In this ever beautiful paradise, I found a new life, I was reborn, as if the curtains were rent asunder, the windows were opened, the doors were unlocked, the walls were removed, the roofs had disappeared. The sun was shedding light; the blue sky had opened its arms to invite the captured birds to fly in its sphere.

The next day we went to a sanctuary a few kilometres from the Gold Coast where a few native animals were kept. For the first time I was able to see these beautiful animals with my own eyes and could pat them with my own hands. I started my life in Australia with the privilege of seeing these beautiful innocent animals. Now my childhood dreams had become a reality. Seeing a kangaroo who nurtures its baby in her pouch under her belly, a koala who carries its baby on its back, the ducklings that follow their mother in the water, and an emu that is a bird, but cannot fly—all these had opened a new world before my eyes.

Wherever I looked, I saw waves of love, kindness and peace. There was no more fear, anguish and worry. The dark, fearful, turbulent years had passed and the gates of hope and freedom were now opened before our faces.

My brother and his wife were very helpful to us and with their help we were able to rent a small townhouse. Now it was time for us to start to build a new life in Australia. We quickly registered our names for English classes. Every day, like primary school students, we would put on our clothes and go to school. Shamim and Basim, who were the younger ones, were learning English much faster and getting used to the new environment.

As for me, even though I had studied English in high school, I still needed a lot more time in order to meet and converse with people. It was often very hard and embarrassing not to be able to explain what I had in mind.

Our new life in Australia, with all its advantages and its regularities, was not free from its own specific difficulties. Cyrus and I, who had left our youth behind, didn't have much energy and it was not easy to start any kind of work or business.

After changing our savings from many years of hard work into US dollars, in those days it was very little. I placed our savings at the disposal of my brother and he, with his own credit, was able to obtain a loan from the bank and build a beautiful house for us on the Gold Coast. We had difficulty in repaying the loan and we decided to sell the house. Fortunately, after a year real estate prices had doubled and we were able to sell the house at a very good price. With the proceeds from the sale of the house we were able to repay the mortgage to the bank and with the profit purchase a nice house in Toowoomba. From that time on the doors of blessings were opened to us and we didn't have to pay rent or mortgage anymore.

After completing his English language course, Shamim entered the Toowoomba University to study construction engineering and, with hard work and perseverance, he successfully finished his course.

As for Basim, who was much younger than Shamim, he completed high school and we moved to Canberra, the capital of Australia. This city has been built in the bushland and it is very beautiful and clean. It has all kinds of facilities, including universities and colleges, and provides the best opportunities for studying science, arts and technology. These institutions are open to everyone who has the necessary prerequisites without any racial, national, or religious prejudices. Basim studied animal science in the Canberra Institute of Technology and, after studying information science, started work.

— — — — — — — — — — — — —

Our life in Australia, like most people, had its ups and downs, its joys and pleasures, its troubles and difficulties, but we had to move forward. Life and living is a constant experience and a learning path. In such a free, secure environment, we were better able to overcome the difficulties and move forward. In other words, the sky here is the same colour as elsewhere, but living under this safe sky is one thing, and living under the insecure sky of my home country, is another. The difference is like heaven and hell.

Under this blue sky they don't imprison birds in cages because of the differences in their colours and bodies, and they never burn their nests. Under this blue sky, they don't strike and whip the budgies and parrots because of their singing, they don't separate the white swans from the black swans, and they don't cover the colourful wings of the butterflies with a black veil.

Under this blue sky they don't stop the movement of the little fish in the sea, they don't chop off the storks' long legs, they don't remove the joeys from the kangaroos' pouches, and they don't stone the beautiful gazelles. (This is a cynical picture of what is happening in my country.)

Under this blue sky, the bountiful rain of God falls equally upon all, the bright sun shines on all, and the ocean breeze refreshes all. They are free to express their thoughts, speak their mind and move freely everywhere.

Under this blue sky the cry of the people does not die in their throats, their chests are not oppressed, their brains are not frozen, their eyes are not blinded with bewilderment, their ears are not closed, their tongues are not dumb, their hands are not tied and their legs are not chained.

Under this blue sky people are alive, under this sky even the dead have the right to be born again!

— — — — — — — — — — — — — —

We planted our roots of existence again in this ever beautiful paradise. We nurtured our roots until they became strong, they grew in all directions, and obtained new forms, new shapes and new memories were created.

My thoughts and my mind soar aloft upon observing the beauties of Australia. My soul flies and unconsciously takes me to the broken, but dormant roots of my existence and remains in the water and soil of my old country. The roots weaken, but they never die. The memories, whether sweet or bitter, lose their shine, but they never fade away.

My faint memories of my old land are always a reminder of those joyous days of my childhood and youth. My heart is nostalgic for that beauty and those sweet moments, I can only recall in my mind and draw in my fantasies.

I am nostalgic for the proud white, magnificent Damavand mountain peak, which never bows.

I am nostalgic for the blue Caspian sea, which slowly swallows the sunset.

I am nostalgic for those dense forests of the north that appear to have hidden some secrets from the sun in their darkness.

I am nostalgic for that salty red desert, ever dry ever thirsty, that keeps its mouth open for a drop of rain.

I wish to hear once again the lovelorn whisper of the desert at night and admire its patience and steadfastness.

I wish to pass once again over the Veresk Bridge and go through Firooz Mountain tunnels.

I wish to move out of the darkness of the tunnels, like children who have hidden themselves there, and run into the foggy light of the mountains.

I wish to see once again the young girls planting rice seedlings in the paddy fields with their flowery petticoats like rotating blooms, flouting side to side. And I wish to inhale the fragrance of the paddies.

I wish to walk once again in the tea plantations and in the cotton fields, become wet from head to toe with the raindrops of the north.

I wish to listen once again to the melodious Gilaki songs, resounding in the air of the north.

I wish to hear once again the roosters' crows in those treed villages, heralding the advent of the dawn and the following sunrise.

I would love to walk once again under the tall plane trees of Pahlavi Street and watch the street pedlar selling fresh walnuts beside his cellular light, waiting for customers.

I would love to watch once again the pedlar roasting corn over a red charcoal fire, soaking it in brine, and to inhale the aroma which has filled the air.

I would love to see Tehran once again in winter, when the whole city is dressed with a cover of snow and watch close up the people who nag and throw snow on the sidewalk from their flat roofs.

I would love to see once again the mature fruitful trees, which have courageously shed their leaves in Tehran's cold winter and gone into dormancy, naked.

I would love to see those yellow allspice flowers pushing themselves out of the snow and smile. I would love to inhale their fragrance once again.

I would love to see Tehran's spring once again with its everlasting Naw-Rúz Festival.

I would love to see the diverse colourful blossoms, inhale their fragrances, become alive with the fervour and excitement which has filled the air and fly with the spring breezes.

I would love to go once again to the crowded noisy Bazaar and look at the great variety of shiny jewellery that is attractively displayed for sale.

I would love to visit once again the chelo kebab (rice and meat cooked over a charcoal fire on skewers) restaurants, and the ice cream shops in the front of the Bazaar. And taste the delicious Iranian foods into my mouth.

I would love to travel once again from the Caspian Sea to the Persian Gulf and pay homage to every foot of that pure land.

I would love to see the people and the lovers of Iran close up once again and kiss their hands and faces and tell them: Although we have each been burned in different ways in the fire of the recent turmoils, we have never lost our identity but have learned a lot.

— — — — — — — — — — — —

It is now nearly 24 years since we arrived in this ever beautiful paradise. My husband Cyrus passed away in 2003 and has commenced his spiritual journey. Shamim and Basim have married and are working. I have five beautiful grandchildren. My house is located at the top of one of the Fadden hills in Canberra.

Every morning I wake up with the sound of the native birds' song in my ears, inviting me to the front balcony. From there I can see the colourful parrots, in groups of twos, and a large group of white cockatoos flying around, and I laugh at the human-like noise of the crows.

The surrounding eucalyptus and pine trees have hidden the neighbouring houses under their canopies and they can hardly be seen. In every direction I look I can see different shades of green. There are two higher ranges behind these low hills that rest on a blue horizon and create a beautiful panorama.

Every day I kiss each of these trees in my thoughts and thank God that the sons and daughters of this land will never suffer the pain and torture we had to bear.

Every day I quietly salute the people and the government of this country, lovers of freedom who have opened their doors to refugees from all over the world, and I bow my head with respect.

Every day my dog Rusty and I go for a walk to the nearby park and watch the grey kangaroos that stand like statues and stare at us. I ask myself, "Am I dreaming or am I awake?" That young girl with the dream of Australia in her mind, who loved to see the kangaroos, is now a grandmother who, after a lot of suffering, has reached peace, safety and tranquillity. Alas, the years of happiness and sadness have passed so quickly!

The question is whether it was the hand of fate and divinity that brought this little girl here or did she herself create her own destiny?

top left, Damavand Peak
top right, Tehran in winter
bottom, Pahlavi Street

Soraya and her father in 1996 in America

Shamim and his wife Hope

Shamim and his children, Adia and Nadim

Basim and his wife Sandra with their children; Kiyanna, Chelsea and Zachary

Three grand-daughters; from left Adia, Kiyanna and Chelsea

Zachary, son of Basim and Sandra

Rusty, Soraya's best pet

Conclusion

Fear and anxiety come and go like a cyclone and in their path uprooting trees, breaking branches and spreading leaves and debris on the ground. Finally it stops somewhere and the dark and ominous clouds make way for the sunshine. The remaining roots sprout, the branches grow along with their leaves.

In conclusion, I wish to thank readers for taking time out to read my story. Perhaps amongst Iranian readers, some have had a similar but less harrowing experience during this tumultuous period of Iran's history. Maybe they have some loved ones or know of others who have lost their lives. Their stories no doubt would most likely be eventful, painful and heart rendering.

I would like to thank Professor, Houshang Khazrai who encouraged me to print and publish my story. I would like to also thank Dr Iraj Master for translating this book and for guiding me through the stages of its publication. Also many thanks to Pilot Hamid Reza Ahmadipour for explaining technical questions about aeroplanes and airports and clarifying any misunderstanding on the subject.

I want to thank my sons Shamim and Basim, who in all situations, remained content and grateful. In all cases they have been supportive to me and dearly value their freedom. I also want to thank my daughter-in-law, Hope Fabillar and dear friend Ms. Carolynne Taylor for their editorial input.

It is also necessary to thank my fellow Baluchi citizens for their honorable help in our flight from Iran to Pakistan. Without their assistance, it would not have been possible for us to cross the borders.

My sincerest gratitude to the people and government of Pakistan who allowed us to stay in their country for nine months.

Finally, I would like to express my appreciation to my Iranian and Australian friends who encouraged me to tell my story, for without their support, this book would never have been written.

Soraya Fathi Bazyar

About the Author

Soraya Fathi Bazyar was born into a righteous family, in 1945 in Tehran. As a child she learned the virtues of family and grew up with love for her country and its rich culture and traditions.

She loved children dearly leading her to a profession in teaching, which she regards as a holy job and a great service to humanity.

After being deprived of human rights in her country, she found solace in Australia in 1985. She started a new life and applied the best points of Australian and Persian cultures to her own life.

Soraya has and continues to offer her assistance as a volunteer worker to newly arriving refugees in Australia, so they can start their new life with ease and settle down comfortably.

One of her strongest beliefs is doing service for humanity. She finds satisfaction in seeing refugees, looking happy after leaving behind a life of turmoil and difficulty. They are the ones who truly appreciate this country.

Soraya is proud to live in a country, that is without discrimination, has human rights and equal opportunities she can appreciate with other Australian citizens. She is very grateful to live in such a peaceful and secure country.

www.ingramcontent.com/pod-product-compliance
Lightning Source LLC
Chambersburg PA
CBHW031300280526
45784CB00004B/1931